JESUS:
ONE MAN, TWO FAITHS
A Dialogue between Christians & Muslims

OTHER BOOKS BY RON MESSIER

Jihad and Its Times
(co-editors, Ronald A. Messier and Hadia Dajani Shakeel)

The Worlds of Ibn Khaldun
(edited by Ronald A. Messier)

The Almoravids and the Meanings of Jihad

To Pam & Mark,
with my best wishes
and God's blessings

Ron Messier

Jesus:
One Man, Two Faiths
A Dialogue between Christians & Muslims

Ron Messier

TWIN
OAKS
PRESS

ISBN-13: 978-0-9844354-4-9
ISBN-10: 0-9844354-4-1

First Edition

Printed in The United States of America

Twin Oaks Press
twinoakspress@gmail.com
www.twinoakspress.com

Cover image of Jesus from Christ Pantocrator Icon (cir. 550) at St. Catherine's Monastery, Sinai Egypt. Note: this Monastery came under the protection of Islam as proclaimed by this document from the Prophet Muhammad.

Cover and Interior design
By Art Growden

To all our children:

Alex, Missy, Samantha, Jody, Ben,

and Mary Elizabeth

Table of Contents

NOTES ON DATES, TRANSLATIONS, AND TRANSLITERATION

All dates are in the Common Era unless otherwise stated.

Translations of the Bible, unless otherwise specified as NIV (New International Version), are from the New American Standard translation. Likewise, translations of the Quran are from Abdallah Yusuf Ali's *The Meaning of the Holy Qur'an* unless otherwise specified. The value of this latter translation for me is to have the Arabic text side by side with the translation, as well as the detailed notes and commentary.

Transliterations of Arabic words into Latin script have been simplified. For example, dots below and above consonants are omitted. Words that are commonly seen in an Anglicized form, such as Quran and jihad, appear in that form and are not italicized. When those words appear in titles of books or articles, they are rendered as they appear in the titles. Names of recent authors are written as the authors render their own names in Latin script.

ACKNOWLEDGMENTS

To name all of the people whose conversations had direct input to the content of this book would be impossible. For those innumerable conversations and the friendships that made them possible and were strengthened by them, I am most thankful. Let me call attention, especially, to four people whose conversations were catalysts to the very idea of writing this. They are: my friend and colleague Rev. Dr. Whitney S. Bodman; my former student, Parwana Ashari; my long-time colleague and archaeology associate, Abdallah Fili; and my archaeology laborer, Ali "the Shoemaker."

The following have read all or parts of the manuscript and have made valuable, insightful comments: the Rev. Colin Ambrose, Dr. Awadh Binhazim, Rev. Dr. Whitney S. Bodman (again), Dr. Allen Hibbard, the Rev. Timothy Jones, Dr. June McCash, Dr. David Rowe, Rabbi Rami Shapiro, and the Rev. James K. Polk Van Zandt. For their considerable contribution of time, effort, and wisdom, I am especially grateful.

My appreciation goes to the Faculty Research Committee at Middle Tennessee State University for granting me a "Non-Instructional Assignment" (sabbatical) for one semester in the very early stages of this project, in the fall of 2003. That grant provided me the opportunity to develop an extensive bibliography and to begin the intensive study of scripture, exegesis, and secondary literature necessary to pursue this topic.

Special thanks go to my designer, Art Growden, for his creative design of the cover and the interior of the book, and to my editor, Nora Hibbard, for her skillful and intelligent editing. Their steadfast dedication to the task has contributed immeasurably to the quality of the final product.

A book like this could not have been written without the support and encouragement of my closest friends, June McCash (again) and Richard Gleaves.

Finally, I would like to thank my very best friend, my wife, Emily, for her love and never ending patience and support in everything that I do.

Chapter One: Introduction

Jesus Is a Jigsaw Puzzle

My family loves jigsaw puzzles. Every Christmas we buy at least two new ones, the largest and most detailed we can find that somehow reflect the seasonal theme. We set them up, usually just one at a time, on a coffee table in the living room, and everyone who comes to the house works on them—at least to some extent. The unwritten rule is that every time a person passes through the living room, that person has to put at least one piece into the puzzle. Gradually, each puzzle gets finished and we marvel at the picture to which we all contributed, a picture with which we were already somewhat familiar; because we had seen it in a smaller version on the cover of the box. Now finished, the picture is much larger; we see the details more clearly because we put it together piece by piece, and it was a communal effort.

I like jigsaw puzzles so much that I use the jigsaw puzzle as a metaphor when I teach historical archaeology. Doing archaeology is like working on a jigsaw puzzle. If you work on puzzles, you can appreciate the challenge of one that has, say, three thousand pieces. It's even more challenging if you don't keep looking at the picture on the cover of the box. Or even harder still, not to mention frustrating, is when some of the pieces are missing. Now, let's imagine that the reason some of the pieces are missing is that the puzzle is very old. But we don't despair because we have found another copy of the puzzle, also very old, also with some of the pieces missing—but hopefully not the same ones.

Getting to know Jesus is, in a lot of ways, like working a jigsaw puzzle—with all of the challenges imaginable. The last time that I taught my class, "Jesus in the Quran," one of the few points that everyone agreed on is that none of us in class knew everything there is to know about God or about Jesus. Some people felt it was possible to know enough about Jesus; but no one felt that anyone could know *everything*. We were working on the puzzle from different boxes. Each person found certain pieces of the puzzle. We might expect that most pieces would be in the Christianity box: pieces for the nativity scene, the miracles, the crucifixion. But, surprising to some students—not so surprising to others—many of the pieces were in the Muslim box, although they sometimes looked different. Some students were willing to consider even other boxes. One student recently had been to the new Museum of the American Indian in Washington DC. He was especially impressed with the section of the museum on Native American spirituality with its focus on our natural environment. He suggested we at least consider that some of the pieces in the nativity scene, for example the clouds, the sky, the animals, the trees, might be in that box.

We decided in class that we would just have to work on this puzzle together. We would have to lay out the pieces in the class room—as many pieces as we could find. We agreed not to get frustrated if there were pieces missing. We would keep looking for them and bring whatever pieces we could find to the table. We agreed that we would not alter any of the pieces to make them fit where they did not seem to belong. In the end, most agreed that the details of the picture were clearer than in any much smaller version on the cover of any one box. There were still some pieces missing, but the picture was beautiful!

PIVOTAL CONVERSATIONS

That Christians could teach Muslims something about Jesus seems obvious to many Christians, but that Muslims could teach Christians something about Jesus might surprise people. Most Muslims know that Jesus is important to them, even though he may not be in the forefront of their religious consciousness. There are scores of books about Jesus in Islam. Do we really need another one? Timing and four specific conversations that I had in recent years made me aware in a very personal way how much Muslims and Christians can learn from each other. So, I decided to write this book.

The first conversation was with Whit, the son of a good friend and colleague. Whit's study of Islam, he told me, had helped him better understand the mystery of the trinity, the Christian belief in three persons in one God. I was intrigued. Whit was enrolled at the time in a PhD program in Islamic studies at Harvard University; he is also a United Church of Christ minister. The conversation moved on to other things before he had a chance to elaborate on this point. In further conversation by e-mail, Whit explained that he had been studying Muslim mysticism and especially the Muslim mystic Ibn al-'Arabi. That particular mystic spoke of God's "locus of manifestation." God in himself is unmanifest, Ibn al-'Arabi taught, unknown, pure light and thus, like the sun, unable to be seen in and of Himself. But God wants to be known, and thus manifests Himself in a variety of ways. The first manifestation can be called God (or Allah in Arabic), the name which includes all other names. Further down the line, Ibn al-'Arabi parses the names of God (traditionally, there are ninety-nine names for God in Islam, but in fact, there are many more) in interesting ways. Each name represents a particular aspect of God. Many of the names form pairs. One can speak of God the life-giver, but also of God the death-giver. These two names balance each other out, as do many others. Each name in these pairs represents an aspect of God, but each alone is unbalanced. To know God, one has to know all the names; mercy has to be balanced with justice, and so on. There are many other names that do not form pairs; they, too, move toward a more complete knowledge of God.

In Christianity, Whit continued, we might think of the Father as the Perfect Master, and the Son as the Perfect Servant, neither of which would be clear without, in some sense, separating them out, just as colors only become clear as they are refracted from white light. When light passes through a prism, it is refracted into the colors of the rainbow; each color is beautiful, distinct from the other colors, visible on its own, but is still part of and inseparable from the same single beam of white light—an excellent metaphor for God.

The second conversation is not quite so complicated. It was with Parwana, a student in my Introduction to Islam course at Vanderbilt University, a course in which close to fifty percent of the students were Muslim; Parwana is Muslim. Among the many topics that we discussed in class was the role of Jesus as it is described in the Quran and in Muslim traditions (*hadith*). Parwana, in one of her essays, described herself as a "highly religious Muslim in nearly every regard... (who) uphold(s) the Quranic verses and *hadith* strictly." To my surprise, she wrote this about Jesus in her final exam: "I find His (Jesus') contribution to Muslim beliefs to be *underestimated* [emphasis mine]," she wrote. "He was one of the most respected and beloved messengers of God and He is the One who will descend on the Day of Resurrection to lead the Muslims in the world against evil....I find it incredible that it is Jesus, not Muhammad, whom the Muslims will follow during the last days of the world. This reinforces my views of Islam as such an adaptive faith." After the course, to my amazement, she came to my office and thanked me for reminding Muslims how important Jesus is to them.

The third conversation was simpler still, but, in one sense, more profound than the others. It was with Ali the shoemaker. Ali and his brothers make and sell shoes for a living. But they also worked as skilled diggers at my archaeological site in Morocco for five to eight weeks at a time during our seasonal excavations. The site is very large with long distances between excavation units. Once in a while, Ali would walk with me from one unit to another—just the two of us. When we had these opportunities to talk alone, we usually talked about God. He was anxious to know what I, a Christian, believed—what I thought about Islam and specific Muslim beliefs—about many spiritual things. And I was curious to know how he, a Muslim, would react to my answers. I clearly remember the day that we talked about jihad. He stressed that the first meaning of jihad, its basic meaning, was not holy war. Most importantly jihad was an inner struggle, within each person, to do good and to avoid evil. He quoted the Quran: "Those who believe, and suffer exile and *strive* (in Arabic, *jahadu*, the root word for jihad) in God's cause with might and main and their persons, have the highest rank in the sight of God" (9:20). Ali asked if Christians had a similar concept. What occurred to me was the passage in Ephesians (6:10–20) where we are asked "to be strong in the Lord and in the strength of His might," to "put on the full armor of God...the breastplate of righteousness" so that we will be able "to stand firm against the schemes of the devil." Another day, we talked about God's infinite love and mercy for His creation. And another day, we talked about Jesus and his mother Mary. He realized that we were not in total agreement here, but still he asked in honest innocence, "Professor, why do we need two religions?" I thought, "Ali, you have done this to me again; you have totally disarmed me." After a silent, deep intake of breath, I answered, "Ali, history is responsible for that." His comeback was, "If all Muslims and Christians could share as we do, the world would be a better place." I put my arms around him and thought to myself that shoemakers are very wise.

Most recently, I met with the director of the Journalists and Writers Foundation in Istanbul that was inspired by, and dedicated to promoting, the philosophy of Fethullah Gülen, a modernist Islamic thinker who encourages intercultural/interfaith dialogue and supports the belief that learning about the other, accepting and respecting the other without surrendering one's own identity, can lead to a more peaceful world. I asked how they promoted that philosophy among people less inclined toward universal dialogue. His answer: "through example and humility, as demonstrated by the prophet Jesus when he washed his disciples' feet."

In short, those four conversations led me to write this book. Timing, also, had a lot to do with it. The events of September 11, 2001 have made us painfully aware that we, as a nation, know very little about Muslims and the Islamic world. I have given more than one hundred and fifty public service presentations in the last six or so years, trying to explain Islam to communities starving to know more about this religion that is described as a religion of peace by some, and yet is used to justify acts of terror by others. Americans have asked many times since 9/11, "Why do they hate us?" Many in the

Islamic world resent certain policies and practices of our government, and some are critical of some of our modes of behavior. But for the vast majority of the 1.6 billion Muslims in the world, those criticisms fall far short of hate. The majority of Muslims feel betrayed by those who commit acts of terror in God's name and in the name of Islam.

Shortly after 9/11, President Bush, in several of his public addresses, made it very clear that he made a distinction between the perpetrators of the crime and Muslims around the world—that the war against terrorism was not a war against Islam. We, as a nation, were under marching orders to respect Islam and Muslims, especially those who were citizens of our country. Many Americans complied, and many did much more, reaching out to learn more about this religion, of which we knew little more than the name, and a few graphic images portrayed in the media connected with specific, mostly violent events. People rushed to bookstores to empty the shelves of books on Islam. Television networks broadcast documentaries about Islam, and various educational, civic, and religious groups sought "experts" on Islam to come to inform their clientele. That is why I did so many lectures beyond my own classes. I sensed, among most groups I spoke to, a real willingness to see similarities between "our" culture and "theirs." So many were surprised to see more similarities than they would ever have expected. But some Americans did not comply, or felt that they could not comply, with President Bush's directives. There were reports of mosques being vandalized and Muslims being attacked in many places across America. Much of the antagonism stemmed from ignorance; some of it was motivated by political considerations that are deflected by religion.

Much more recently, President Barack Obama re-launched this outreach to the Muslim world. He did it in Cairo, on their turf, more directly, more forcefully, and hopefully with greater success than previous administrations.

It would be fair to say up front where I am coming from in writing this book. I am a retired professor of Islamic history and archaeology, having first taught at Middle Tennessee State University and then at Vanderbilt. I am still active in research and writing. I have been studying Islam for a very long time, since I was an undergraduate in college over forty years ago. Before that, I had had a lot of exposure to Christian education. I grew up Roman Catholic and attended Catholic schools from kindergarten through two years of college. I think it is fair to say that the primary source for that religious education was the Baltimore Catechism, more important perhaps than the Bible itself. We read the Bible, of course, and scripture readings were incorporated into the liturgy. But doctrines described in the Baltimore Catechism were based on what was called tradition as well as on the Bible. "Tradition," in that context, means the writings of the fathers of the church and other theologians as well as practice as it evolved in the church over the ages. This is not so different than Islam, really, which places a lot of importance on traditions (*hadith*) in addition to the divine scripture of the Quran. In fact, there are more sayings attributed to Jesus in Arabic than in any other language.[1] Jewish tradition and Jewish commentary on scripture is no less important to consider, to be sure, but I must confess that I have much less exposure to that tradition other than some reading and a few mini classes. So, I cannot claim to add a Jewish perspective to my narrative.

The events of September 11, 2001 precipitated a turning point in my approach to scripture. My close friend Bob invited me to enroll in an internationally syndicated Bible study program. Like so many others, I felt out of touch with my own feelings at this time of crisis. I was groping for some kind of explanation for what had happened and for some source of comfort. I also wanted to spend time with Bob, so I went. We spent the next nine months studying Moses in the Old Testament, and scripture began to take on a whole new meaning. I spent four years studying with that Bible study group. In the process, I was overtaken by the power and the beauty of what I saw, in some sense, as the revealed word of God. I have become convinced that scripture, both the Bible and the Quran, has to be the very foundation for what we can learn about God—and about Jesus. I have also spent a lot of time reading exegetical writings, commentaries on scripture, both Muslim and Christian. These have been most useful in learning how those two traditions have evolved in slightly different ways, in different historical contexts, by separate cultures, often leading to what appears as contradiction of one religious tradition by another.

Most recently, I completed a four-year course of theological study, Education for [lay] Ministry (EFM), offered by the School of Theology at the University of the South. The first year focuses on the Old Testament, year two on the New Testament, year three on Church History, and year four on Theological Choices. The program is best characterized, as I think is Anglican Christianity in general, as being a safe place to explore one's own spirituality. The program certainly offered me sound content in the areas listed, as well as experience in thinking theologically, with enough latitude to explore—as I have in the pages that follow.

Finally, I hope to share what I have learned from so many of my friends, Christian and Muslim, as well as what I have learned from many years of formal study of both religious traditions. My thinking has been shaped by the

1. Houston Smith, "Jesus and the World's Religions," In *Jesus at 2000*, ed. Marcus J. Borg (Boulder and Oxford: Westview Press, 1998), 108.

many conversations that I have had over the years, especially in the last two or three years, with Muslims and Christians all over the world.

DO CHRISTIANS AND MUSLIMS WORSHIP THE SAME GOD?

In the New Testament book of Acts, we read: "I most certainly understand now that God is not one to show partiality, but in every nation the man who fears Him and does what is right, is welcome to Him" (Acts 10:34–35). The Quran says that God gives the following assurance to all believers: "Those too who believe what has been revealed to you, and what has been revealed before you [Jewish and Christian scripture], and who know for certain that there is an afterlife, these are truly guided by their Lord; these are truly saved" (Quran 2:4–5, Khalidi translation).

Although there are differences in how Christians and Muslims understand the unity of God (trinity vs. triunity vs. unity—a question to be taken up later), the Muslim answer to this question is without hesitation "yes" because the Quran reveals it to be so. The God of the Quran is the God of Abraham, Isaac, and Jacob, the same God as the God of the Bible. The well-known Muslim theologian Seyyed Hossein Nasr echoes this idea when he says, "Despite the difference of emphasis in the two religions, namely the insistence of Christians upon trinity and of Muslims on unity, it is not difficult to reach an accord on the ultimate nature of God, the One Reality."[2] The Christian answer has been more ambiguous. The canon of the Bible was closed several hundred years before the Quran appeared, so it obviously does not mention Islam by name. The eighth-century church father John of Damascus, an Arab Christian who lived under the protection of the Islamic court of the Umayyads in Damascus and worked for the caliph, saw Islam as a Christian heresy but still answered the question "yes." So did Pope Gregory VII, the Cluniac Reform pope who, ironically, set much of the stage for the First Crusade in the late eleventh century. In a letter to a Muslim prince in Africa, Pope Gregory said, "Although in a different manner, we believe and confess the one true God."[3] This letter was cited in the document of Vatican II which added, "Those also can attain to everlasting salvation who through no fault of their own do not know the gospel of Christ or his Church, yet sincerely seek God and, moved by grace, strive by their deeds to do his will as it is known to them through the dictates of conscience" (II, 16, 35). The sentiment has been ignored for centuries. Then as now, many have answered the question "no."

2. Seyyed Hossein Nasr, "Comments on a Few Theological Issues in the Islamic–Christian Dialogue," in Yvonne Yazbeck Haddad and Wadi Z. Haddad, *Christian–Muslim Encounters* (Gainesville: University Press of Florida, 1995), 457–58.

3. Julius Basetti-Sani, "For a Dialogue between Christians and Muslims," *Muslim World* 57 (1967): 130–31.

Do Muslim and Christian scriptures in fact contradict each other? When reduced to absolute truth statements, it appears that they do. Take, for instance, the belief that Jesus is the only begotten Son of God as is stated in the Nicene Creed and based on the New Testament verses Acts 13:33, Hebrews 1:5 and 5:5, "You are my Son; today I have begotten You." What exactly does *beget* mean here? When Christians say that Jesus is the only begotten Son of God, are they thinking of the father–son relationship in literal terms of biological DNA? The Quranic response to this is, "It is not befitting to the majesty of God that he should *beget* [emphasis added] a son" (Quran 19:35). Muslims reject the idea of God engaging in the physical act of begetting. I think most Christians would agree. In either case, can the father–son relationship be a way of describing the uniquely special relationship between God "the father" and Jesus?

The crucifixion is another issue where Christian and Muslim scriptures seem to directly contradict each other. Christian scripture states unequivocally that, "the soldiers took charge of Jesus. Carrying his own cross, he went out to the place of the skull....Here they crucified Him..." (John 19:16–18, NIV). On this, all of the gospels agree. But the Quran says: "they [the Jews] killed him not nor crucified him but so it was made to appear to them" (Quran 4:157). Many Muslims see this as an explicit denial of the crucifixion. But what does this verse require Muslims to believe? What if the question were shifted from whether or not Jesus was crucified to the identity of the agent of the crucifixion? In other words, maybe it wasn't the Jews who killed Jesus, maybe it was the Romans, or maybe it was everyone who ever committed an evil deed, as at least one Muslim scholar suggests.[4] We will revisit both of these issues, as well as many others, in separate chapters. What do these contradictions, or apparent contradictions, really mean? Do the respective belief statements, simply put, reveal all of the texture that their scriptures offer?

What about scriptures that appear specifically to exclude the other, scriptures like, "Thomas said to Him, 'Lord, we do not know where you are going, how do we know the way?' Jesus said to him, 'I am the way, and the truth, and the life; no one comes to the Father, but through me'" (John 14:5–6), and "there is salvation in no one else [other than Jesus]; for there is no other name under heaven that has been given among men, by which we must be saved" (Acts 4:12). In much the same way, the Quran appears to exclude non-Muslims: "And this day have I perfected your religion" (Quran 5:3). Reading these verses might lead a believer to say, "I have the truth. You

---

4. M. Kamel Hussein, *The City of Wrong: A Friday in Jerusalem*, trans. Kenneth Cragg (Oxford: Oneworld, 1994).

don't. Therefore, you need what I have." This gives rise to what we might call "conflicting truth claims." But we can think about the issue of truth in different ways?

FACTUAL/HISTORICAL TRUTH AND MYTHICAL TRUTH

What we know based on fact, based on empirical evidence, what is recognized by all to be true because there is irrefutable, observable, recordable evidence, we normally accept as "true." It is a fact that the Boston Red Sox baseball team finally won the World Series in the year 2004. There were millions of eye witnesses who observed, and none contested what they saw. Myths, on the other hand, are often thought to be not true—only myths. The very thought of mythical truth seems somewhat of an oxymoron. But to understand myths as true, we have to think about truth in a different way than we might have so far. I gained an interesting insight into thinking about truth in a new way when I read Andrew Greeley's book, *The Sinai Myth*.[5] When considering the biblical events on Mount Sinai, Moses receiving the Ten Commandments, we can ask at least two very different kinds of questions about these events. We can ask historical or factual questions like "when did it happen?" or "where did it happen?" or "how did it happen?" These are very interesting and very important questions, but questions to which we have very unsatisfactory answers. There is a rather wide chronological window within which these events may have taken place, anywhere from around 1450 to 1200 BC. We know that they occurred on Mount Sinai, but there are at least two Mount Sinais in the Sinai Peninsula. Which one was it?

The "how" question may be the most difficult one of all. Did God actually write the words of the commandments on the two stone tablets? What did God's voice actually sound like? If Moses had had a tape recorder, would it have recorded anything? We cannot answer these questions on the basis of historical evidence.

So what happens if we ask a different kind of question, a mythical question? What is the significance of whatever took place on Mount Sinai? Could it be that the mythical truth, the significance and ultimate reality of those events, is that from this time on (whenever exactly that time was), because of whatever happened on Mount Sinai (wherever that may be), the Hebrew nation entered into a new relationship with whom they accepted God to be, and that relationship was based on law, on the covenant? The nation accepted the conditions spelled out in the commandments in exchange for God's promise to deliver them into the promised land.

Christmas is another myth. We could ask the same kinds of questions

5. Andrew M. Greeley, *The Sinai Myth* (Garden City, NY: Doubleday, 1972).

about the birth of Jesus: "When did it happen?" "Where did it happen?" How did it happen?" The time-frame window here is much narrower than for Moses on Mount Sinai, but still not precise, sometime between 6 BC and AD 4. Was the manger exactly on the silver star embedded in the floor of the Church of the Nativity in Bethlehem? It would be nice to think so. How did it happen? We will take up that question in some detail in our discussion of the virgin birth of Jesus. Historically, the answers to these questions about Jesus are more precise than those about Moses, but still not as precise as many would like them to be.

So what is the mythical truth of Christmas? What is the real meaning of the birth of Jesus? Is it the way, or at least one of the ways, many believe that God chose to make Himself known to humankind? Christians believe that it is part of the story of redemption. Myths help us understand things for which we have little or no empirical data. Myths may not be factually true; they may even be factually false. Still, they have communicated over generations something that cannot be expressed by "mere" facts, something of enduring and widespread significance.

LOGICAL TRUTH AND FAITH BASED/SCRIPTURAL TRUTH

Logical truth is what we know to be true because we concluded it to be true based on known facts. We have already accepted as fact that the Boston Red Sox won the 2004 World Series, so we can logically conclude that the "Curse of the Babe," the curse that they would never win another World Series because of selling Babe Ruth to the New York Yankees in 1920, had now been broken.

Faith based truth, on the other hand, does not have to be based on empirical evidence. Rather, it is based on some source of authority, like sacred scripture. It involves believing that the source of authority speaks the truth. The Latin word to believe (*credere*), refers to an act of will rather than an act of reason, albeit reason would not necessarily be excluded. Christian scripture gives a good definition of faith. It is "the assurance of things hoped for, the conviction of things not seen" (Hebrews 11:1). Faith is equally a cornerstone in the Muslim approach to understanding God. The first of the Five Pillars of Islam is the profession of faith: "There is no God but God, and Muhammad is his prophet." Quran 2:3–4 stresses that those "who believe in the Unseen are steadfast in prayer and spend out of what We [God] have provided for them. And who believe in the Revelation sent to thee and sent before thy time and (in their hearts) have the assurance of the Hereafter."

To accept something as an act of faith involves wanting or choosing to accept something as true. It is not test tube knowledge, but rather the kind of knowledge that is based on trust or love. Dr. S. Wesley Ariarajah, a Methodist minister from Sri Lanka who served on the staff of the World Council of Churches during the 1980s, provides a good example of a non-religious faith statement: his little girl believing that her daddy is the very best daddy in the world. She is honest about it; she knows no other person in the role of her father. There is no doubt about it in her mind. When she says, "My daddy is the best daddy in the world," she is speaking the truth. But she is also speaking in a language of faith and love. Ariarajah admits that the statement would probably not hold up under empirical scrutiny. He knows men who are better fathers. "The language of the Bible," says Ariarajah, "is also the language of faith....The problem begins," he adds, "when we take these confessions in the language of faith and love and turn them into absolute truths."[6]

ABSOLUTE TRUTH AND CONTEXTUAL TRUTH

Is Dr. Ariarajah's daughter guilty of relativising truth? Does that take something away from the very nature of truth? Does it make truth totally subjective to the person stating the truth? If all truth is relative or subjective, then does absolute truth just evaporate away? Let's try changing the term "subjective truth" to "contextual truth." You might reject this idea in the end, but at least think about it. To me, contextual truth is something that is either true or not within a certain context. For example, it is true that radar speed detectors are illegal in Kentucky, but it is not true that they are illegal in Tennessee. What about the story of Noah and the flood in the Bible, could that be an example of a contextual truth? After forty days and forty nights of rain, the Bible says that the "whole world" was covered by the deluge. The whole world in which context? The world that Noah knew? The world known by the Jews at the time that the Bible was actually written down? The world as we know it today? These are three very different worlds. Still another possibility for understanding the flood story could be the difference between literal truth and allegorical truth. When I once said that "my aunt Tilly weighs a ton," I did not literally mean two thousand pounds. It was pure hyperbole.

What about the biblical passage, John 14:6? Here Jesus says to his disciples, "I am the way and the truth and the life." Could this apply to anyone who strives to live a life in the way that Jesus led his life? To live a life according to the principles that Jesus taught in his beatitudes, parables, and in the two great commandments? And the next phrase, "No one comes to the Father except through me. If you really knew me, you would know my Father as well." Does "no one" here mean among Jesus' disciples, no one among Jews

6. Charles Kimball, *Striving Together: A Way Forward in Christian-Muslim Relations* (Maryknoll, NY: Orbis Books, 1991), 65.

in first-century Palestine, no one anywhere ever? In accepting these words to be true, are Christians bound by faith to deny salvation to all who have never heard of Jesus or who do not know Jesus as Lord and Savior?

One Saturday morning, a visitor to our Bible study class explained it this way. Imagine that one day God decided to buy *everyone* a Coca Cola. All one had to do to benefit from the offer, to enjoy the Coca Cola, was to accept it. I recently used this metaphor in a discussion with one of my students in my class on Islam. As we talked, a new twist in the offer developed. God doesn't offer Cokes to people directly. He does it through intermediaries. Someone delivers the message or makes the offer in God's name. The intermediary even packages the offer somehow to make it deliverable, even attractive, in a bright red can or easily recognizable bottle. But what if the intermediary offering the Coke poured it from the can into a frosted glass or a paper cup? What if, as was done in a commercial for another brand of cola, two drinks were put in neutral containers. Would the consumer be able to tell the difference? Would the person who accepted a Coke in a container supplied by the intermediary benefit from the drink, get the nourishment of the drink, or even just the flavor of the drink, if he or she did not know that this was "Coke"?

Do we have to know the name of a benefactor to benefit from his gift? When I was a child, one of my favorite television shows was *The Millionaire*. Each week, the wealthy philanthropist gave a gift of one million dollars to a designated recipient. The point of the program was to see how the gift would be used. The only stipulation for the recipient was that the gift had to remain anonymous. The recipient never knew who the wealthy philanthropist was, but he/she still got the million dollars, still benefited from the precious gift, still became a millionaire.

Does the New Testament insist that everyone know the name of the donor? When God sent Jesus as a sign to the whole world, did he mean just those to whom someone told Jesus' name? Many Christians say "yes." But some disagree. Referring to John 14:6, the Episcopal EFM Manual says:

> This saying has troubled many over the centuries and has been used to justify the condemnation of "unbelievers," but its reference is entirely within the community of disciples. Jesus is telling his disciples what their roots and guarantees are, not ruling out the "pagans"—or, for that matter, the "Jews."[7]

Kenneth Cracknell, a Methodist scholar in England, suggests approaching the passage John 14:6 as a contextual truth. He suggests thinking about it in

7. EFM (*Education for Ministry*) Year Two: *The New Testament*, 4th ed. (Sewanee, TN: The University of the South, 2000), 209.

the context of the four main theological points of the Gospel of John: 1) Jesus is one person, 2) Jesus is truly human, 3) Jesus is truly divine, and 4) Jesus is ultimately related to the action, presence, and revelation of God here on earth throughout human history.[8] This fourth point is what the Gospel of John calls the Word, *Logos* in the Greek scripture. How Christians sought to work out the relationship among these four elements and what they ultimately mean was and remains not easy. We will discuss that more in detail when we talk about the trinity. In the meantime, Cracknell suggests focusing on Jesus as the *Logos*. Jesus' statement is actually a response to questions posed by Thomas. Basically, Thomas wanted to know the way; he wanted to know exactly what it was that Jesus wanted him to do. Muslims, incidentally, want to know the same thing. Their scripture shows them the *shariah* which also means the way. But the Gospel of John personalizes "the way" differently than other religions by making it synonymous with Jesus, Jesus as *Logos*. Jesus is the way, or one of the ways, that God reveals himself to human beings, the way God draws humans to Himself. But Cracknell warns against casually reducing the rich words of Jesus to a set of simple, static, absolute, theological propositions. When Peter said in Acts 4:12 that "there is salvation in no one else; for there is no other name under heaven that has been given among men by which we must be saved," we have to bear in mind, Cracknell argues, to whom Peter is talking. Cracknell stresses that this statement has to be seen from a Christian perspective. *For the Christian*, there is no other name. Christians must, by definition, affirm the healing, redeeming work of God through Jesus. This is an affirmation of what God means *to Christians*. It does not refer, according to Cracknell, what God is *not* doing where the name of Jesus is not known in exactly the same way, much less where Jesus' name is not even known at all. It is *contextually* true for those Christians who know Jesus' name, who understand Jesus in a certain way, that no one comes to God except through him.

In the broader context of all four gospels, does it not appear that Jesus meant to include outsiders rather than exclude them? In John 10:16, for example, Jesus says, "And I have other sheep, which are not of this fold; I must bring them also, and they will hear My voice; and they will become one flock with one shepherd." In the next chapter, John 11:51–52, the high priest prophesied that "Jesus was going to die for the nation, and not for the nation only, but in order that He might also gather together into one the children of God who are scattered abroad." Just whom is he talking about here?

In the same way, we have to look at Muslim scripture contextually. For example when we read: "But when the forbidden months are past then fight

8. Kimball, *Striving Together*, 66–67.

and slay the pagans wherever ye find them and seize them, beleaguer them
and lie in wait for them in every stratagem (of war)" (Quran 9:5), it seems
to exclude or to reject all non-Muslims. But this is not true if you look at the
context of the passage. First of all, the verse would not apply to Christians or
Jews, of course, because neither of these were considered pagan. But even if
it did, a broader context is needed to understand the meaning. The context
is presented in the verses that immediately precede the one quoted. The
question is raised as to what is to be done if the enemy breaks faith and is
guilty of treachery. The answer given is that a period of four months' grace
be established to allow the violators of the treaty an opportunity to return to
compliance. We should also read on to the second part of the verse and the
verse after that:

> but if they repent and establish regular prayers and practice regular
> charity then open the way for them: for God is oft-forgiving most
> merciful.
> If one amongst the pagans ask thee for asylum grant it to him so that
> he may hear the word of God and then escort him to where he can
> be secure: that is because they are men without knowledge (Quran
> 9:5–6).

Later on in the same chapter, verse 29 does apply specifically to Christians
and Jews:

> Fight those who believe not in God nor the Last Day nor hold that
> forbidden which hath been forbidden by God and his apostle nor
> acknowledge the religion of truth (even if they are) of the People of
> the Book until they pay the *jizyah* with willing submission and feel
> themselves subdued.

Jizyah is a form of tax collected from non-Muslim People of the Book—those
who believe in Jewish and Christian scriptures. The tax is rarely collected in
today's world, but in the days of early Islamic theocracies, it was collected.
People of the Book had to accept the jurisdiction of the state just as Muslims
did. They had to pay this tax both as a symbol of this submission and as a
substitute for serving in the armed forces. They enjoyed rights of citizenship,
but were not liable for service to the state as were Muslim citizens.

Yet another quotation that sometimes causes alarm:

> O ye who believe! take not the Jews and the Christians for your
> friends and protectors: they are but friends and protectors to each
> other. And he amongst you that turns to them (for friendship) is of

them. Verily God guideth not a people unjust (Quran 5:51).

Reading this in the original Arabic might provide a more conciliatory meaning. The word *awliya*, translated here as "friendship," really means much more than that. It means protection. Another verse, Quran 3:28, cautioned Muslims, back in the era when Islam was struggling to become established, to seek protection from other Muslims rather than from any non-Muslim group. The context is that of an age when tolerance of one group by another was not normally offered—and not expected.

Back to the truth issue. Are there absolute truths, things that are categorically true, always and in every circumstance? Probably. I, personally, am inclined to say "yes." The difficulty is in knowing which "truths" to recognize as such. People of faith rely on divine revelation to know absolute truth. But even here, interpretation comes into play. People see divine revelation differently depending on their own situation, their own perspective. Azar Nafisi, author of the best selling book *Reading Lolita in Tehran*,[9] describes how she explained this point in her classroom using a chair. She placed a chair in the room and asked a student to describe it. She then turned the chair upside down and asked a different student to describe that. Then she asked students in different places in the room to describe the chair. Each student described it differently. The chair was the same, but students saw it differently. Some of her students, those she described as Islamists, were as certain of their absolute truths as any person of any faith is certain of what they know from divine revelation. What is absolute truth, by definition, in divine revelation doesn't change, can't change. But people who look at it might see it differently, depending on where they are standing or sitting in the room, or in the larger world.

My approach is based on three assumptions/conclusions. First, both the Bible and the Quran are in some sense "revealed scriptures." We will explore what that means in the next chapter. Second, both scriptures are subject to interpretation in the sense that, as soon as anyone thinks that a statement—any statement—means something, that's interpretation. We will examine closely the role of human interpretation in both Christian and Muslim scripture also in the next chapter. Third, the views of Jesus in Christianity and in Islam are not the same, but when one steps back, at least for a moment, from absolute truth statements and closely examines the texture of what both scriptures say, the images of Jesus are more complementary than contradictory. At times when two truth statements seem contradictory, real dialogue can point toward a third possibility where some common ground exists.

The goal is *not* to show that Muslim and Christian beliefs are the same.

9. Azar Nafisi, *Reading Lolita in Tehran: A Memoir in Books* (Random House, 2003), 198–99.

They are not. Christians are virtually unanimous in believing that Jesus is God, even if it is difficult for many to explain how. On the other hand, no Muslim could ever say that Jesus is God. Nor is the goal to minimize the differences between the two religions for the sake of peace. That would be unfair to one, or more likely, to both religions. Nor is the goal to show that one tradition is true and the other is not. The goal is *not* to convert anyone from one faith to another, or to get anyone to surrender those beliefs that are fundamental to their own spirituality. The goal is, rather, to show that, although it can be difficult and asks a lot from both Christians and Muslims, it is possible for people of both faiths to dialogue with each other, even about God, and that Jesus can be the focus of that dialogue. The pages that follow invite believers of each faith to reflect on their own images of Jesus and, perhaps, expand those images in light of what the other has to offer. I sometimes find myself expanding some of those images—some Christian images and some Muslim images—toward each other, but hopefully not beyond the boundaries allowed by scripture. As one might expect, on any particular point of discussion, on any particular concept, one would not expect *all* Christians to agree or *all* Muslims to agree. The goal is to find overlap in concepts on which at least *some* Christians and *some* Muslims would agree.

OVERVIEW

Since context is important, Chapter Two will present the historical context. It will talk about sources. It will talk about how scripture became scripture, how both the Bible and the Quran became canonized texts. It will paint, at least in broad brush strokes, those events in the early history of Christianity and Islam that affected how early Christians and early Muslims developed images of Jesus. From there, we will proceed more or less chronologically through the life of Jesus. Chapter Three will present the birth narratives in both Christian and Muslim traditions. The story of Jesus' birth is remarkably similar in both traditions, but we will see some differences. Not only do the new details that show up in the Muslim narratives give a little more information, they show that the Muslim narratives are not merely imitating the earlier Christian narratives. Chapter Four will describe the public ministry of Jesus. It is the story of Jesus the miracle worker, Jesus the perfect servant. Does Jesus perform the same miracles in both traditions? How is it and why is it that Jesus performs miracles in the first place? Again, there are some differences, but the similarities are striking. In both traditions, Jesus is seen as the perfect servant and, in both, the perfect servant becomes a suffering servant. Here, the story at first glance separates in the two traditions. In Christianity, the perfect servant is sacrificed, crucified to atone for the sins of humanity. This is potentially one of the most serious conflicts in interpretation between Christianity and Islam; but a closer look is warranted. Chapter Five will look very closely at the crucifixion narratives and will consider a range of interpretations in scriptural commentary, bearing in mind that one absolute truth cannot contradict another. Chapter Six will examine both Christian and Muslim views of sin and atonement. Chapter Seven is about the resurrection and the second coming; it was my student Parwana who put me on to new insights about this. Those are the events that form the narrative of the story. But always in the background is the issue of the trinity, the Christian mystery of three persons in one god, the issue of the humanity and the divinity of Jesus, and the relationship between the two. When Christians think about God the Father and Jesus as his only begotten Son, what exactly does "Father" mean in this context? When Muslims say that God does not beget nor is begotten, what does the word "beget" mean to them? What role does the Holy Spirit, or the Spirit of God as the Quran phrases it, play in both traditions? Potentially, these questions are the most divisive between Christianity and Islam. We will pick up certain pieces of the puzzle that we have already laid out in the preceding chapters and put them together in Chapter Eight to address these questions. How Christians and Muslims relate to God is the subject of Chapter Nine. How personal is the relationship? How do they pray? Could they conceivably pray together?

CHAPTER TWO

Revelation—When God Speaks, People Listen

THE HISTORICAL CONTEXT OF DIVINE REVELATION

When God told Adam that he was dust (Genesis 3:19), that was not the final word. Time and again, God, through his prophets, told the story of rebellion, judgment, repentance, and redemption. After many centuries, some heard God to say that Jesus was a prophet, but also much more; that he was the Messiah, the Word made flesh, the agent of redemption. After several centuries more, Muslims believe that God told the prophet Muhammad to recite his word to the people of Arabia. If God spoke through all of these prophets, was he not speaking to all of mankind? Why repeat himself over and over again, century after century from Adam to Muhammad? In successive revelations? Would not what God said in one time and place apply to all others? Is divine revelation so time sensitive? Is it not universal? Are the Bible and the Quran competing scriptures? At first thought, they may seem to be so, but the relationship is too complex to be answered with a simple yes or no. We have to take into account the immediate circumstances of the specific populations who were the first to hear these revealed words. God chose to deliver his message through intermediaries. Even if God intended his revelation to be accepted by all, he had to use words and arguments that were immediately relevant to the population at hand who were hearing these words for the first time. Otherwise, the message would have been dropped on the spot and would have gone no further. God would have failed to reveal himself altogether.

Often enough in the past, Christians and Muslims have been decidedly negative in how they perceived the relationship between the two faiths. Much of the negativism or disagreement that we find separating Christianity and Islam was developed in the heat of battle, battle first among the various groups within Christianity, each struggling to put forth its own Christology, mostly during the fourth, fifth, and sixth centuries; then, battle among Muslims struggling to define their own belief system; and finally, battle between Muslims and Christians in the period leading up to and then during the Crusades. But even in this most heated of confrontations, as we have already seen, Pope Gregory VII, the pope who was at the very forefront of the reform ethos that contributed directly to crusader ideology, was able to say of both Christians and Muslims: "Although in a different manner, we believe and confess the one true God."[1]

CANONICAL SCRIPTURE

The main source for Christian perceptions of Jesus is the Bible. But how did the Bible come to be? Most Christians accept the Bible as a compilation of many books, sixty-six for Protestants, seventy-three for Catholics, and seventy-six for Orthodox Christians. These books were written by some forty different authors over a period of fifteen hundred years. But over time, these books became bound into a single book. Christians often describe the Bible as "the Word of God." They believe that the Bible is divinely inspired, but they mean different things by that. Some, a minority perhaps, believe in direct, verbal inspiration, that is, that the authors were passive recipients of the divine word, that God dictated word for word, and the scripture writers wrote it down exactly as God said it. Others believe that God superintended the process, but allowed individual authors to use their own style and words to compose and record the message that God wanted us to know. In either case, God *revealed* the message. To reveal literally means to unveil, to make known what would otherwise remain unknown. God had a message he wanted to make known to people on earth. The Bible was a means to make that message known.

What the Bible claims for itself is that "all Scripture is inspired [literally God-breathed] by God" (2 Timothy 3:16); "...no prophecy was ever made by an act of human will, but men moved by the Holy Spirit spoke from God" (2 Peter 1:21). Prophecy that appears in the Bible through this process is not subject to error, save for human error.

The canon of the Hebrew Bible was well established by the time that Jesus lived. Jesus was called "Rabbi" several times in the Gospel of John (1:38, 1:49, 3:2, 3:26, 6:25) which according to John 1:38 means "teacher" of scripture. Jesus was quite familiar with scripture (should anyone be surprised?). He debated scripture with the Pharisees, who knew scripture all so well, and quoted the Old Testament with ease. When asked which commandments

---

1. Quoted in Julius Basetti-Sani, "For a Dialogue," 130–31. Gregory wrote this in a letter to the Muslim Prince Anzir in Mauritania. Implied in what Gregory says is that God's grace also applies to non-Muslims.

were the most important to follow, he quoted several from Exodus 20. But then added, quoting Deuteronomy 6:5, "You shall love the Lord your God with all your heart and with all your soul and with all your might," and quoting from Leviticus 19:18, "...love your neighbor as yourself" (Matthew 19:19). By the time that Jesus lived, there was, for the most part, no debate as to which books made up the canon of the Old Testament.

The New Testament, on the other hand, obviously came into being after Jesus' death. What books were ultimately included among the twenty-seven books of the New Testament as it exists today was determined by applying four criteria. First, they had to be apostolic, written by an apostle or at least by a companion of an apostle. The four gospels, the primary biographies of Jesus, are traditionally attributed, and there is some disagreement about this,[2] to the apostles Matthew and John, and companions of the apostles Luke (traveling companion of Paul) and Mark (secretary of Peter). In the narrow sense of actually being written by an apostle, many of the books of the New Testament are not apostolic. But in the broader sense of containing "apostolic teaching" as defined by the emerging church of the early centuries, the Testament is apostolic.[3]

New Testament books had to be catholic in the sense of universal, that is, they had to have had continuous acceptance and usage by the church at large. They had to be orthodox in the sense that they conformed to the rule of faith, meaning that they were congruent with the basic tradition that the "established" churches recognized as normative.[4] A good example of a book that did not meet this test is the Gospel of Thomas. In it, Jesus says, "Split wood; I am there. Lift up a stone, and you will find me there." That is pantheism and is contrary to the teaching of the canonical New Testament.[5] So, it did not make the final cut. Finally, the books had to be "ancient," written near the time of Jesus. Most of the books that finally were accepted into the canon were written during the first century AD. The earliest letters of Paul were written in the middle of the first century, and 2 Peter, thought to be the final New Testament book to be written, was written around 120. There are other books that were written during this period that did not make

2. Bart D. Ehrman, *Lost Christianities: The Battle for Scripture and the Faiths We Never Knew* (New York: Oxford University Press, 2003), 235, says that most scholars today have abandoned the traditional identification of the authors and believe that the books were written by otherwise unknown authors.

3. Ibid., 236.

4. Ehrman calls these "established" teachings proto-orthodox, i.e., views that are expressed in the formative years of the church that will ultimately be accepted as orthodox by creedal decree.

5. Lee Strobel, *The Case for Christ: A Journalist's Personal Investigation of the Evidence for Jesus* (Grand Rapids, MI: Zondervan, 1998), 68.

the final cut, but all those that did make it were written within ninety years of Jesus' death. Most of the books that were considered controversial and did not make it into the canon were written sometime after 120.

In 120, the issue of which books would be included and which would not was far from resolved. But by the end of the second century, the present New Testament canon was virtually agreed upon. What's more, sometime in the second half of the second century, a creed for use at baptism had been framed to oppose particular doctrines such as Gnosticism. It came to be called the Apostles' Creed in accordance with the criterion of orthodoxy, that is, apostolic. It says:

> I believe in God the Father Almighty; *maker of heaven and earth* [later added to make a point against the Gnostics]; and in Jesus Christ, his only begotten Son, our Lord, who was born of the Holy Spirit and the Virgin Mary, crucified under Pontius Pilate and buried; the third day he rose from the dead, ascended into heaven, being seated at the right hand of the Father, whence he shall come to judge the living and the dead; and in the Holy Spirit, holy Church, forgiveness of sins, and the resurrection of the flesh.

The first written statement that we have listing all twenty-seven books of the New Testament as canonical was written in 367. It is a letter written by Athanasius, bishop of Alexandria, who wrote a letter once a year to the churches in Egypt under his jurisdiction. He wrote these letters first of all to announce the date for Easter (which was not established in advance as it is today) and also to give pastoral advice to the souls under his care. In his famous thirty-ninth letter, he lists the books that his flock should accept as revelation: the books of the Old Testament including the Old Testament Apocrypha and the twenty-seven books of the New Testament as we know it today.[6] At this point, no church council or synod had declared a canonical bible. Rather, the list reflects widespread consensus, the intuitive insight of a critical mass of Christian believers. Athanasius's list was endorsed before the end of the century by St. Augustine, bishop of the North African Diocese of Hippo, perhaps the greatest orthodox theologian of antiquity. Augustine pushed its acceptance at the Synod of Hippo in 393. And we know that because its proceedings were summarized at the Synod of Carthage four years later:

> The canonical Scriptures are these [there follows a list of the books of

6. Ehrman, *Lost Christianities*, 230.

the Old Testament]. Of the New Testament: the gospels, four books; the Acts of the Apostles, one book; the epistles of Paul, thirteen; of the same to the Hebrews, one Epistle; of Peter, two; of John, apostle, three; of James one; of Jude, one; the Revelation of John. Concerning the confirmation of this canon, the church across the sea shall be consulted.[7]

The "church across the sea," that is, the Church of Rome, was consulted and concurred. That the process took over a quarter of a century shows how much care was taken to ultimately decide what was divinely inspired and what was not. A canon would have been useful much earlier to ward off competing claims, and presumably false claims, to divine inspiration and orthodoxy. But deciding on a canon simply took time and resulted, in large part, from interaction with groups that would ultimately be called heretical.

CHRISTIANITY IN THE PRE-ISLAMIC ERA

The Christian world, both east and west, at the time of the early Christological controversies, was dominated by the Byzantine Empire, sometimes called the Christian Roman Empire. By the late sixth and early seventh centuries, the Byzantine Empire was not especially tolerant toward religious beliefs that differed from the "official" creed of the state. To be a Christian, at least in the eastern part of the empire, meant in some sense to be subject to the Byzantine Empire. This would certainly have been an obstacle for Arabs at that time to accept an orthodox Christian perception of Christ. W. Montgomery Watt tells us that, for the sake of their trading interest, it was important for the Arabs to maintain neutrality between the Byzantine and the Sassanid Persian Empires.[8]

Another handicap faced by early Christians trying to grasp an understanding of Christ's relationship to God was the labyrinth of abstractions supporting one or another of the various Christologies of the day, abstractions whose relevance was hard to discern by the average lay person. What exactly is an *ousia* (essence/being)? or a *hypostasis* (substance)? The question is further complicated by the fact that different church fathers used the terms in different ways. Sometimes *hypostasis* was used to mean *ousia*. The issue became even more confused when the Greek terms were translated into Latin, and the meanings shifted a little more.

The discussions begin to make a little more sense when one asks *why* the protagonists of one position or another advanced the arguments that

7. Quoted in Ehrman, *Lost Christianities*, 246.
8. William Montgomery Watt, *Muslim-Christian Encounters: Perceptions and Misperceptions* (London: Routledge, 1991), 7.

they did. What was the historical and cultural background in which the various Christologies developed? What was the chief problem of human life that a particular position tried to resolve? History and culture explain a lot. For example, ancient Egyptian culture was one that was obsessed with overcoming human mortality. The great lengths to which ancient Egyptian embalmers went to mummify a deceased human body testifies to that. The virtual absence of change in artistic style—the pyramids themselves—strive for permanence here on earth. The fact that the pharaoh died in every generation was a flaw in this quest for permanence. So the ancient Egyptians made the pharaoh a god. More than that, they merged the collective identity of deceased pharaohs with the god Osiris, chief god of the underworld, and the collective identity of living pharaohs with Horus, son of Osiris. This is a rather mystical concept, and the structure breaks down when one tries to submit it to logical explanation.

It is in this very Egyptian environment that the idea of Christ having a single divine nature (Monophysitism) emerged.[9] Although he was no Monophysite himself, the basis for this belief comes from none other than Athanasius, bishop of Alexandria. According to Athanasius, Jesus Christ is the incarnation of the divine Word; his human nature becomes incorruptible and is resurrected after death. Furthermore, Jesus accepts the penalty of death for all of sinful humanity. Through association with the body of Christ, Christians share in this incorruptibility. Through Christ, humans achieve everlasting life. The Monophysite twist conceptualizes a single divine–human nature, a union of the divine word with human nature. The divine nature dominates since the human nature, by association with the divine nature, becomes incorruptible. This is a way of Christianizing the Ancient Egyptian preoccupation with death and escaping from it. Monophysitism differs from the official Byzantine position, and I might add from Athanasius himself, in that the Greeks maintained that Christ is at the same time fully divine and fully human, that these two natures are totally separate, distinct, and coexistent. This position is called Diophysite and is the position of most Christians today.

In Western Syria, Monophysitism developed for a different reason. For many people there, the great problem for human beings was the attainment of material security in this life. The patriarch of Antioch, Severus (d. 538), taught that human suffering and hardship was God's punishment for sin, but it was also God's way to call his servants to a better life. Severus saw

9. See Watt, *Muslim-Christian Encounters*, 4–5.

God as *energia*, "power in action."[10] Accordingly, he saw Jesus as a divine–human *energia*. Christians could obtain this energy through the Eucharist, the celebration or reenactment of the miracle of the incarnation. Divine power manifests itself through human life. This could not be done if human and divine natures remained separate. The two natures had to merge into one divine nature.

Still another variant of this idea is Gnosticism. The Gnostics started by separating all material things from the spiritual world. They regarded the material world as so degrading that God could have had nothing to do with making it. A more radical form of Gnosticism, called Docetism, claimed that when Jesus came into this vile and material world to save it, he came in the masquerade of a body, but his flesh could not have been real; it only appeared to be real. Furthermore, since God cannot suffer, it only *appeared* that Jesus suffered, and it only *appeared* that he died on the cross. We will discuss this idea further in the chapter on the crucifixion.

The central point for East Syrians, also known as Nestorians, was that God is eternal, unchanging, with no beginning and no end. They believed that Jesus did indeed have two natures, human and divine, but these two natures operated quite separately. On Christmas Day, 428, Nestorius, the patriarch, provoked a riot among the monks of Constantinople when he preached:

> They ask whether Mary may be called God-bearer. But had God, then, a mother?...Mary did not bear God...the creature did not bear the Creator, but the man, who is the instrument of the Godhead. The Holy Spirit did not place the Word, but He provided for Him, from the blessed Virgin, a temple which He might inhabit...He who was formed in the womb of Mary was not God Himself, but God assumed him.[11]

Nestorius said that the Jesus of history had a complete human nature, endowed with reason and free will, like all other human beings; and the divine *Logos* dwelt in him as in a temple, in perfect moral unity, such that the *Logos* and Jesus willed the same things. He believed that Mary gave birth to the human body of Jesus, but not to the divine Word. Centuries later, Timothy, the Nestorian patriarch in Baghdad, met with the Abbasid Caliph. He explained the death of Jesus by saying that it was only the "human nature of the Word-God which suffered and died, because in no book of the prophets

10. Ibid.
11. Quoted by Warren H. Carroll, *The Building of Christendom: A History of Christendom*, vol.2 (Front Royal, VA: Christendom College Press, 1987), 92.

of the Gospel do we find that God died in the flesh. The expression that God 'suffered in the flesh' is not correct."[12]

EARLY CHRISTIAN INFLUENCE IN ARABIA BEFORE ISLAM[13]

The population in Arabia on the eve of Islam was, for the most part, pagan. The residents were fiercely independent and would not have been inclined to accept Christianity because to do so risked subjecting themselves to control of Byzantine imperialism. But there were some Christians in Arabia. One legend, albeit not widely reported, says that inside the Kaaba, a religious shrine in Mecca long before Islam, were pictures of Jesus and Mary, along with the black stones representing pre-Islamic, pagan deities.   And a Christian Arab poet wrote on the eve of Islam, "In the name of the lord of Mecca and of the Crucifix." He saw the Christian God and the Muslim God as one and the same. There were Christian merchants from Syria who passed through, Christian slaves brought in from Abyssinia, and Christian refugees fleeing persecution from Byzantine intolerance. But these Christians, especially in the latter case, would not have been orthodox Christians. Those Christians who came to Arabia were mostly Monophysites and Nestorians. It stands to reason that when Arabs converted to Christianity, and they did in small number, they would accept one of these Christologies. It has even been suggested that the Quran's image of Jesus echoes Nestorian criticism of orthodox Christian belief.[14] Remember, the Nestorians separate Jesus' human nature from the divine. Additionally, there were even small groups of "Christian Jews," converts to Christianity from a Jewish background, who could accept Jesus as Messiah but not as a divine being.

As far as we know, there was no Arabic translation of the Bible at the time of Muhammad, except maybe for short, isolated passages stowed away in some Christian monastery or similar place. On the other hand, we know that many of the foreign words in the Quran are of Aramaic derivation.[15]

We learn in an early biography of Muhammad[16] that while traveling to Syria as a young boy with his uncle, he met the Christian monk Bahira in the town of Bostra. The ruins of the Nestorian church where this meeting allegedly took place can still be seen today in the city. The story goes that the

---

12. Quoted by Geoffrey Parrinder, *Jesus in the Qur'an* (Oxford: One World Press, 1995), 118.
13. The information for this section comes from Neal Robinson, *Christ in Islam and Christianity* (Albany: State University of New York, 1991), 17–22 and W. M. Watt, *Muslim-Christian Encounters*, 6–7.
14. Robinson, *Christ in Islam*, 21.
15. Arthur Jeffery, *The Foreign Vocabulary of the Qur'an* (Boston: Brill, 2006).
16. A. Guillaume, *The Life of Muhammad: A Translation of Ibn Ishaq's Sirat Rasul Allah* (Oxford: Oxford University Press, 1955).

monk recognized that the boy was a prophet and advised the uncle to take special care of him. There is no evidence beyond legend that Bahira taught Muhammad anything about Christianity.

The cousin of Muhammad's wife Khadija, on the other hand, a man named Waraqa, was a Christian. According to a well-known tradition, Waraqa, now old and blind, had been able to read and write Hebrew letters and had actually translated part of the Hebrew Bible. When Muhammad received his first revelation, he was so frightened as to what it all meant that Khadija advised him to visit her cousin Waraqa. This is what Waraqa said: "How I wish that I could be alive when your fellow citizens banish you!" "So they will drive me out?" cried the Prophet. "Yes," retorted Waraqa, "no man has ever brought what you bring without being persecuted."[17] Waraqa saw Muhammad's experience as a prophetic revelation like those of the prophets of the Bible. It was the first of many for Muhammad. They would accumulate to produce the Holy Quran.

One cannot overstate the importance of Muhammad to Muslims. Waraqa, a Christian, recognized him for who he was, the man who brought the word of God to a body of believers who would become known as Muslims. As a prophet, he "is 'the touchstone of Islamic identity and loyalty,' the focus of love and devotion, and the ideal model for Muslims."[18]

THE REVELATION AND CANONIZATION OF THE QURAN

Whereas the Bible was revealed over a period of some fifteen hundred years to several different authors, Muslims believe that the Quran was revealed word for word, God's word, directly to Muhammad by the Holy Spirit, or the Spirit of God, all within a period of twenty-two years.

> Say the Holy Spirit has brought the revelation from thy Lord
> In truth, in order to strengthen those who believe, and as a Guide
> and glad tidings to Muslims (Quran 16:102).

The Holy Spirit (*Ruh al-Qudus* in Arabic) in this case spoke through the angel Gabriel.[19] Quran 2:97 specifically identifies Gabriel as the messenger who brings God's revelation to earth. Quran 16:2 says that God sent down his angels with inspiration of his command. The word translated here as "inspiration" is *ruh* which more literally translates as "spirit" or "breath." This

17. Reported by Sahih Bukhari, quoted by Robinson, *Christ in Islam*, 24.
18. Zoe Herzov, citing Kenneth Cragg in "Translator's Afterward," Ali Merad, *Christian Hermit in an Islamic World: A Muslim's View of Charles de Foucauld,* (Mahwah, NJ: Paulist Press, 1999), 97.
19. Abdullah Yusuf Ali, 664, note 2141.

association of Gabriel being the messenger with God's "inspiration" itself (*ruh*) is, perhaps, what lead several classical exegetes to identify the Holy Spirit, at least in some contexts, as Gabriel.[20]

The language of the revelation is "Arabic pure and clear" (Quran 16:103). The Quran does not describe the process itself, but Muhammad through his biographer said, "Never once did I receive a revelation without thinking that my soul had been torn away from me."[21] Sometimes Muhammad saw Gabriel in the form of a man, and he could hear the words clearly, but "sometimes it comes unto me like the reverberations of a bell, and that is the hardest upon me; the reverberations abate when I am aware of their message."[22] In these situations, Muhammad apparently turned inward, searching his own soul for a solution or meaning. This is exactly what God, in the Quran, told him to do when he said, "Move not thy tongue with it to hasten it. Ours is to gather it, and to recite it, follow thou its recitation. Then ours it is to explain it" (Quran 75:16–19).

Muslims see this phase of divine revelation to be part of the same continuum of revelation which began with God revealing himself to Abraham. A good friend, who is at the same time a biblical archaeologist and a Church of Christ minister, explained it to me this way: God began to reveal himself to the Hebrews almost four thousand years ago. They accepted the divine revelation, but they did not actively spread it. Two thousand years later, it had still not spread very far. Proselytizing is not a Jewish thing. So God tried a second time by sending Jesus. Christians were more effective in spreading the word; but by the late sixth century, this divine revelation still had a long way to go. So God tried yet again by revealing himself in Arabic in the Arabian desert. This time God chose Arabic for these revelations because he was revealing himself to Arabs.

The period before these revelations began to come to Muhammad is known as *jahiliya* (the period of ignorance). There was a sense among many Arabs of a lack of a scriptural tradition. They knew that Jews and Christians had scriptures of their own. Why not the Arabs?

> And this is a Book which We have revealed as a blessing: so follow it
> And be righteous, that ye may receive mercy. Lest ye should say: "The
> Book was sent down to two Peoples before us, And for our part, we

20. Ibn Kathir, *Tafsir Ibn Kathir*, Abridged, vol. 7 (Riyad: Darussalam Publishers & Distributors, 2000), 275–276.

21. From Ibn Ishaq, quoted by Karen Armstrong, *Muhammad: A Biography of the Prophet* (San Francisco: HarperCollins, 1992), 83.

22. Ibid.

remained unacquainted with all that they learned by assiduous study
(Quran 6:155–156).

It appears that Muhammad sought advice from others to find the
meaning of these revelations. We have already seen that he went to his wife's
cousin, a Christian, to resolve his earliest doubts. He apparently tried to
consult Christians, but he did not have direct access to earlier scriptures. The
Quran says:

> Say: "Who then sent down the Book which Moses brought?—
> A light and guidance to man: But ye make it into (separate) sheets
> for show,
> While ye conceal much of its contents (Quran 6:91).

All Muslims believe that the entire Quran was revealed to Muhammad,
and that the prophet established the divisions and the order of the chapters
(*suras*) before he died. It is said that Gabriel came to Muhammad every year
during the process of revelation to have him recite the Quran and make
corrections. The Quran itself reveals that changes were indeed made during
Muhammad's lifetime: "For every verse We abrogate or cause to be forgotten,
We bring down one better or similar" (Quran 2:106, Khalidi translation). In
the last year of his life, it is said, Gabriel had Muhammad recite the entire
Quran twice to make sure he had it right. Many Muslims had committed all
of the revelations to memory. Much of it had been written down, even if only
in pieces and scratched onto palm branches, scraps of wood, or thin stones.
Those who believed that Muhammad received divine revelation pressed him
to give them a book too. "No, we shall not even believe in thy mounting [to
heaven to meet God] until thou send down to us a book that we can read"
(Quran 17:93). It is possible that Muhammad did write down many of the
verses, or, more likely, recited them so one or more of his copyists could write
them down.

There are different stories about who compiled the first complete written
Quran.[23] A common belief is that the first caliph, Abu Bakr, did it. This
would have been within the first two years after the prophet's death. As the
story goes, he was prompted to do this by Umar Ibn al-Khattab who became
concerned that so many reciters of the Quran, companions of the prophet
who had memorized the Quran during the prophet's lifetime, had been killed
at the battle of al-Yammama in 632, just after the death of the Prophet. So he
suggested to the caliph that he commission the compilation of one complete

23. For a narrative of the various traditions, see *Encyclopaedia of Islam*, 2nd ed. (EI2), vol. 5, 404–5.

Quran, so that none of the revelation would be lost. He commissioned one of the prophet's secretaries, Zayd ibn Thabit, with the task. Zayd collected all of the fragments that were written on stones or leaves or pieces of wood and tested these against the memories of the companions of the prophet. He wrote all of the verses on sheets of equal size. When Abu Bakr died, Umar succeeded him and acquired the written Quran. He, in turn, passed it on to his daughter Hafsa, a widow of the prophet.

Another version of the story says that the third caliph, Uthman, was the one who produced the canon of the Quran. This story says that there was a dispute between Muslim forces from Iraq and Syria over the correct way of reciting the Quran during communal prayers while they were on the march. One of the generals reported the problem to the caliph. So Uthman obtained the "sheets" from Hafsa and appointed a commission under the direction of Zayd ibn Thabit. They produced several copies of the "official" version, one to remain in Medina and others to be sent to Mecca, Kufa, Basra, and Damascus. All other copies or portions were to be destroyed. Reportedly they were—except in Kufa, where one Ibn Mas'ud and his followers refused until threatened with force.

What we can be confident of is that the Quran that we have today, at least in terms of the number and arrangement of the chapters and the basic structure of the text, does go back to Uthman, to the middle of his reign, to approximately 650–52 twenty years after the prophet's death. We know that Zayd ibn Thabit, the prophet's main secretary, played an important role in compiling the canon of the Quran; and we know that this text was deemed official. Vowel markers would be added to this text about a hundred and fifty years later.

THE HUMAN ROLE IN DIVINE REVELATION

Communication involves both transmission and reception. In the case of sacred scripture, both Christians and Muslims accept God as the transmitter. Prophets are the receivers. Prophets then relay the divine message to the rest of the community. Whether or not the message is accepted as valid then depends on a consensus of a critical mass within the community. God is the source of what is revealed in scripture, but humans played an indispensable role in the process of its communication. God must have wanted it that way.

In a Bible study group that I participate in, we have often debated what exactly was meant by a particular passage. We often wondered as a group, "Why doesn't God just say it plain and simple? Why doesn't He just lay it out there in a way that is not ambiguous, that is straight forward and easy to grasp with absolute certainty?" One answer is that some things—important things—are just not plain and simple or unambiguous. For God to make them plain and simple would take something away from the precision of it. Those of us who are parents who have at one time or another helped our children with homework can appreciate God's dilemma. When helping a child learn something, were you ever tempted just to make it easy for the child and solve the problem for him or her? To simply give guidance and then watch the child struggle to find the answer takes far more patience—and love, but in the end will produce much more learning on the part of the child. God so loves humankind that He chose to involve humans directly in the process of divine revelation, to give humans an integral role in receiving the divine word, transmitting it to others, and in the end in struggling to learn what it all means.

There is an interesting passage in the Quran in which God chooses Adam above the angels to understand the intricacies of divine revelation:

> Behold thy Lord said to the angels: "I will create a vicegerent on earth." They said "Wilt thou place therein one who will make mischief therein and shed blood? Whilst we do celebrate Thy praises and glorify Thy holy (name)?" He said: "I know what ye know not."
> And He taught Adam the nature of all things; then He placed them before the angels and said: "Tell Me the nature of these if ye are right."
> They said: "Glory to Thee of knowledge we have none save that Thou hast taught us: in truth it is Thou who art perfect in knowledge and wisdom."
> He said: "O Adam! tell them their natures." When he had told them God said: "Did I not tell you that I know the secrets of heaven and earth and I know what ye reveal and what ye conceal?"
> And behold We said to the angels: "Bow down to Adam"; and they bowed down. Not so Iblis, he refused and was haughty, he was of those who reject Faith (Quran 2:30–35).

When God taught Adam the "nature of all things," he revealed to Adam the inner nature and qualities of things, divine revelation. But it wasn't all that easy, neither for Adam nor for Eve. The footnote to verse 30 in Abdallah Yusuf Ali's translation of the Quran is particularly interesting:

> It would seem that the angels, though holy and pure, and endued with power from God, yet represented only one side of Creation. We may imagine them without passion or emotion, of which the highest flower is love. If man was to be endued with

emotions, those emotions would lead him to the highest and drag him to the lowest. The power of will or choosing would have to go with them, in order that man might steer his own bark.... The angels in their one-sidedness saw only the mischief consequent on the misuse of the emotional nature by man; perhaps they also, being without emotions, did not understand the whole of God's nature, which gives and asks for love.

It is the reciprocal love between God and humankind that explains the human role in receiving divine revelation. In the very next chapter of the Quran, God says: "Say: "If ye do love God follow me: God will love you and forgive you your sins for God is Oft-Forgiving Most Merciful" (Quran 3:31). Likewise, the Bible is replete with references of God's love for humankind. "God so loved the world that He gave His only begotten Son" (John 3:16). God so loves the world that he will help us with our homework, but he will not do it for us.

CHAPTER THREE

For Unto Us a Child Is Born

During the summer of 2008, I had the opportunity to visit the House of the Virgin Mary near Ephesus in modern Turkey. How do we know that it was really the house of the Virgin Mary? Here is the evidence that suggests that it was. We know that the apostle John went to Ephesus after the crucifixion. We read in the Gospel of John that Jesus said to John: "'Behold, your mother!' From that hour the disciple took her into his own household" John 19:27). That scripture supports a strong tradition that John did indeed take Mary to live in Ephesus after Jesus ascended to heaven, a tradition that seems to be supported by a letter written by the members of the Council of Ephesus held in 431 to the clergy of Constantinople which said: "We reached the city of Ephesus where John the Theologian and the Mother of God, the Holy Virgin, were separated from the assembly of the holy Fathers".[1]

A nineteenth-century German mystic, Anna Katharina Emmerich, described a series of visions in writing that became *The Life of the Virgin Mary*. In the last two chapters, the visionary recounts that Mary came to live near Ephesus in a house provided her by Saint John. The German mystic, who had never left Germany in her entire life, described her vision of the house itself in minute detail, as well as the site, the surrounding countryside, and distance from Ephesus. Her description fits what we saw to a tee. Parts of the foundation of the house were dated to the first and fourth centuries, with still another part of the house dating to the seventh.

Whether the House of the Virgin Mary that tourists and pilgrims visit today is the actual house that Mary lived in or died in may be less important than the fact that pilgrims do come—Christian pilgrims *and* Muslim pilgrims. They merge into a single-file line to pass through the tiny, humble stone house where they believe that Mary lived.

1. *Catholic Encyclopedia*, "Tomb of the Blessed Virgin Mary," http://www.newadvent.org/cathen/14774a.htm.

Let's look first at the birth narratives in the gospels. The Christmas story, as it is sometimes called, appears only in the synoptic Gospels of Matthew and Luke. A good chain-linked Bible will provide links from one book to another where there are similarities or elaborations to what is revealed. For example, in the margin of Matthew 1:21 where the angel of the Lord announces the birth of Jesus to a virgin, there is a link to Luke 1:31 where the angel makes the same announcement. But like so many stories in the gospels, this one is significantly different in each account. Nowhere is this clearer than in the listing of the genealogy of Jesus in Matthew 1:1–16 and in Luke 3:23–38. Genealogies in the Bible are long lists of names that are, for the most part, rather unfamiliar to us today. I find reading these lists somewhat boring, so boring that I tend to skim right over them. Perhaps that's why I didn't notice at first that the genealogy in Matthew's account is not the same as the one in Luke's account. I was at least mildly disturbed. How are we to know what Jesus' real genealogy is? Doesn't God know?

One explanation for the discrepancy between the two genealogies is that Matthew provides the genealogy of Jesus through his adoptive father Joseph's line on the one hand, and that Luke, on the other hand, gives us the genealogy through the line of Mary, although he doesn't tell us that. This explanation is not without problems. Biblical scholar James D. Tabor explains it this way. Luke identifies the generation before Jesus with the words: "He was the son, *so it was thought* [emphasis added] of Joseph" (Luke 3:23, NIV). This raises the question of the identity of Jesus' real father, the issue of the "virgin birth." Most people back then assumed that Joseph was the father. We will come back to that. Tabor provides the freely paraphrased translation of Luke 3:23 as: "And Jesus was about thirty years old when he began his work, *supposedly* being a son of Joseph but *actually* being of the line of Heli."[2] Who was Heli? Tradition says that Mary's parents were Joachim and Anna. Tabor suggests that Heli is short for Eliakim, which in turn is another form of Joachim. Tabor further suggests that Luke leaves Mary's name out of the genealogy in keeping with the ancient Hebrew tradition of including only male names in the list. Tabor makes several other interesting observations about these genealogies. But the point to make here about the two different genealogies is that one gospel does not contradict the other. Rather, the two complement each other. Together, they provide a more complete family tree for Jesus both on his legal father's side and on his biological mother's side. Both were descendants of King David. But Tabor also points to the important fact that in the genealogy in Luke—Mary's genealogy—there are several links

2. James D. Tabor, *The Jesus Dynasty* (New York: Simon & Schuster, 2006), 52.

to the priestly line of Levi. Mary's genealogy not only links Jesus to the kingly line of David, but also to the priestly line of Levi. This is corroborated by Mary's relationship to her cousin Elizabeth, also a descendant of the priestly line of Levi, and Elizabeth's husband Zacharia who was in fact a priest in that line. The Quran upholds this link as well. Quran 3:35 says: "Behold! a woman [Hanna/Anna, Mary's mother] of Imran said: 'my Lord! I do dedicate unto thee what is in my womb for Thy special service so accept this of me for Thou hearest and knowest all things.'" Imran is Arabic for Amram, the father of Moses, Aaron, and Miriam, and the grandson of Levi.

The story of the birth of Jesus begins in the Gospel of Luke with God sending the archangel Gabriel to Nazareth, a town in Galilee, to a virgin engaged to be married to a man named Joseph. The virgin's name was Mary. The angel said to her that she had found favor with God, and that she would become pregnant and give birth to a child. She was told to call him Jesus, and that he would be great and would inherit the throne of David. Astonished and confused, Mary said, "How will this be since I am a virgin?" The angel said, "The Holy Spirit will come upon you, and the power of the Most High will overshadow you." In other words, she would become pregnant by the power of God, the Holy Spirit. The annunciation is quite different in the Gospel of Matthew. The angel of God, who remains unnamed in this gospel, appeared to Joseph rather than Mary. They were already engaged; he knew that she was pregnant and that he was not the father of the child. This is an embarrassing situation in any culture, but especially so in the Middle East, in ancient times as today. So what was Joseph to do? The angel told him that the baby was conceived by the power of the Holy Spirit, as foretold by the prophet Isaiah, and that he should go ahead with the wedding. He agreed. But going back to the Gospel of Luke, Mary hurriedly traveled to the small town of Ain Karem to visit her cousin Elizabeth. She allegedly went to assist her cousin in childbirth as she, too, was pregnant—with John the Baptist. But she might also have gone to conceal the embarrassment of her own pregnancy. Luke tells us that Mary and Joseph were engaged to be married when they traveled to Bethlehem where Jesus was born (Luke 3:5). Tabor takes this to mean that they were not married until after Jesus was born.[3]

The Quran is a third scriptural source for the Christmas story. Like the gospels do for each other, it complements the two gospel accounts and adds interesting details and insights. It would be useful, actually, if someday someone would produce a chain-linked Bible–Quran, with links from the Bible to the Quran and back again.[4] We should not expect the Quran to give

3. Ibid., 44.

4. Dr. Brian Arthur Brown, a minister in the United Church of Canada and author of *Noah's Other Son: Bridging the Gap between the Bible and the Qur'an*, is in the process of doing this.

as much space to the story of Jesus as does the gospels, not because Jesus is less important to Muslims, but rather because the gospels have already told the story. The Quran echoes some details of the story in confirmation, and adds other details. "It is he (God) who sent down to thee (step by step) in truth the Book confirming what went before it; and he sent down the Law (Of Moses) and the Gospel (of Jesus) before this as a guide to mankind" (Quran 3:3). The Quran, like the Gospels of Matthew and Luke, tells the story of the annunciation in *sura* 19, the Sura of Maryam (Arabic for Mary):

> Relate in the Book (the story of) Mary when she withdrew from her family to a place in the East.
> She placed a screen (to screen herself) from them: then We sent to her Our angel and he appeared before her as a man in all respects.
> She said: "I seek refuge from thee to (God) Most Gracious: (come not near) if thou dost fear God."
> He said: "Nay I am only a messenger from thy Lord (to announce) to thee the gift of a holy son."
> She said: "How shall I have a son seeing that no man has touched me and I am not unchaste?"
> He said: "So (it will be): thy Lord saith 'That is easy for Me: and (We wish) to appoint him as a Sign unto men and a Mercy from Us': it is a matter (so) decreed."
> So she conceived him and she retired with him to a remote place (Quran 19:16–22).

As in the Gospel of Matthew, here the angel remains unnamed, although Muslim tradition assumes that it is Gabriel. Quran 21:91 and Quran 66:12 both say, "We breathed into her of Our Spirit [*Ruh*]." Two early Muslim commentators on the Quran, Al-Tabari and al-Baidawi, both said that the angel of God, Gabriel, identified as the *Ruh,* breathed or blew into her garment so that she conceived. The Prophet Muhammad's early biographer, Ibn Ishaq, spoke of "Mary the virgin, the good, the pure."[5] Following the Gospel of Luke rather than Matthew, the angel appears to Mary, rather than to Joseph. In fact, Joseph does not appear in the Christmas story at all in the Quran.

What is clear in all three versions of the story, though, is that this baby was conceived not in the normal way of intercourse with a man but through the intercession of God through the Holy Spirit in Christianity or "Our Spirit" (*Ruhina*) in Islam. All three scriptural accounts agree on this. In fact, the Quran is so emphatic about Mary guarding her chastity that it says: "It is

5. Parrinder, *Jesus in the Qur'an*, 61.

not befitting to (the majesty of) God that he should beget a son. Glory be to him! When he determines a matter, he only says to it 'Be' and it is" (Quran 19:35). This is interpreted by many Muslims as an emphatic denial that God had intercourse with Mary in order for her to conceive this special child. The note to this verse in Abdallah Yusuf Ali's translation of the Quran reads: "Begetting a son is a physical act depending on the needs of men's animal nature. God Most High is independent of all needs, and it is derogatory to him to attribute such an act to him. It is merely a relic of pagan and anthropomorphic materialist superstitions." This is a sticky issue in Islam. The Arabic word for "beget" in Quran 112:3, "He begetteth not, nor is begotten," is *walada*, which clearly means the sexual act of begetting or bearing a child. The Arabic word for "beget" in Quran 19:35, on the other hand, is *ittakhadha* (to make). Combined, as it is, with the word "son," it could have a sexual meaning, but it also might not. It is ambiguous. The important point here, though, is that most Muslims, and I would add Christians, would agree that Jesus' conception was not the result of a sexual act on the part of God and the virgin Mary, but rather as a result of a command on the part of God.

The virgin birth is something that transcends our normal understanding of things. Of course, there is any number of things that we do not understand scientifically, but that we believe anyway. But somehow, the virgin birth of Jesus is different, harder for some to accept. This is a good place to begin dialogue among Christians and Muslims, though, because the mainstream of both traditions believes that Jesus was conceived solely by the will of God. That said, it is quite clear that there are many skeptics of the virgin birth of Jesus. That should come as no surprise. The common assumption is that all human beings have both a biological mother and a biological father. And Muslims and Christians alike believe that Jesus was human. Interestingly enough, there seem to be far more skeptics among Christians than among Muslims. There are some skeptics among Muslims to be sure; Geoffrey Parrinder names at least four modern Muslim writers who deny the virgin birth: Sayyid Ahmed Khan, Tawfiq Sidqi, Parwez, and Muhammad Ali.[6] But, personally, I have never met a Muslim who denied the virgin birth of Jesus. Some of my Christian friends are very skeptical of it; some who attend church regularly, some who attend Sunday school classes, some who teach Sunday school classes, reject it altogether.

Some reject it on scientific grounds. The argument is that a child just cannot normally be conceived that way. The counter argument is that that is precisely the point. This is not a normal occurrence. This is God's doing.

6. Ibid., 69–70.

If you take God out of it, it couldn't happen. If you take God out of it, the whole question of the virgin birth is a moot point. It is a matter of faith, and faith and science operate in two separate realms. But let's take faith out of the picture for a moment and think of it just from the point of view of science. A virgin birth would certainly be a scientific anomaly. But more and more often, it seems, science is coming up with something new, forcing us to rethink what we have "always" or traditionally held to be true and forcing us, sometimes, to accept new "truths." Thomas S. Kuhn in his *Structure of Scientific Revolutions*[7] explains how this happens. What people see depends both on what they look at and on what their previous visual–conceptual experience has *taught* them to see. That is called a paradigm. Discovery begins with the awareness of an anomaly, the recognition that nature has violated the paradigm-induced expectations that govern normal science. Anomalies can be ignored, denied, or unacknowledged; or they can be explored, which might lead to a new paradigm. An obvious example would be the shift from believing in an earth-centered universe to a sun-centered solar system. In recent times, Nobel Prizes in chemistry or physics have been awarded to scientists whose discoveries lead to paradigm changes. Most people don't believe that chimerical beings, centaurs, mermaids, and the like, exist in real life. They exist only in Greek myths and seamen's tales. But in 1972, Paul Berg's laboratory at Stanford University succeeded in inserting viral DNA into a simian virus (SV40), thereby creating a chimerical virus. Shortly thereafter, it became possible to create all sorts of genetic chimeras like laboratory mice with human genes. Berg won a Nobel Prize for that work in 1980.[8] This is not to suggest that science will someday come up with an explanation for the virgin birth. It is to suggest that it is not entirely illogical to accept a particular occurrence without a scientific explanation.

People of faith believe that to produce the anomaly of a virgin birth is not beyond God's unlimited power. The Ahmadiyya sect of Islam explains it this way: "Whereas Islam recognizes the virgin birth of Jesus as a miraculous event, it does not consider it unnatural; the laws of nature are never broken. It just reflects the inability of man to fully understand the science behind various phenomena observed in nature."[9] To think that God cannot act outside of a paradigm formed by humans is contradictory to the infinite power of the divine.

7. Thomas S. Kuhn, *The Structure of Scientific Revolutions*, 3rd ed. (Chicago: University of Chicago Press, 1996).

8. D. Peter Snustad and Michael J. Simmons, *Principles of Genetics*, 4th ed. (Hoboken, NJ: John Wiley & Sons, 2006), 421 and 508.

9. Waseem, "Jesus Son of Mary..... Beliefs of (Ahmadiyya) Muslims," http://www.city-data.com/forum/religion-philosophy/141379-jesus-son-mary-beliefs-ahmadiyya-muslims.html.

Other skeptics or critics question or reject the virgin birth by putting it in the same category as other miraculous birth stories in ancient mythology. There is actually one example in a Hindu Purana where a god impregnates a virgin by artificial insemination, he tells her, so as "to keep your virginity intact, since you are still an unmarried girl."[10] But most of these myths involve impregnation by the male seed of a god who somehow managed to seduce the maiden. We have already stressed that both Christian and Muslim traditions agree that Mary did not become pregnant by some masculine physical act on the part of God, that Jesus was not begotten by God in that literal, physical sense of the word as is the case in Greco–Roman myths. Noted Biblical scholar James D. Tabor writes: "When you read the account of Mary's unsuspected pregnancy, what is particularly notable in both (gospel) texts is an underlying tone of realism that runs through the narratives. These seem to be real people, living in real times and places. In contrast, the birth stories common in Greco–Roman literature have a decidedly legendary flavor to them."[11]

Some people suggest that the term "virgin" is inappropriately applied to Mary. This argument is based on the reference in the Gospel of Matthew (1:22–23) to the Old Testament prophecy in Isaiah 7:14: "Now all this took place to fulfill what was spoken by the Lord through the prophet: 'Behold, the virgin shall be with child and shall bear a son, and they shall call his name 'Emmanuel,'" which translated means, "*God with us.*" The Hebrew word that is translated as "virgin" in Matthew 1:23 is *'alma,* which in most Old Testament contexts is translated as "young woman" or "maiden." A more specific Hebrew word for "virgin" is *bethulah.* But, since young, unmarried women, maidens, were expected to be virgins, "virgin" could be an acceptable translation for *'alma.* In fact, the Septuagint translators, a panel of Hebrew scholars and Jewish rabbis, more than two hundred years before the birth of Jesus, having no inherent belief in the virgin birth, translated *'alma* in Isaiah 7:14 with the Greek word *parthenos,* the specific word for "virgin." They had decided that if *'alma* could mean "virgin," in the context of Isaiah 7:14, it did mean precisely that. If, possibly, there is ambiguity in the use of the term "virgin" in the Bible, there is none in the Quran. The Quran is very explicit, consistent, and unambiguous about the term "virgin" and about the virgin birth, which explains why so many Muslims accept it. In Islam, Mary is set apart from all other women: "Behold! the angels said: 'O Mary! God hath chosen thee and purified thee; chosen thee above the women of all nations'" (Quran 3:42). Many Muslims argue that Mary remained sinless.

10. *Bhāgavata Purāna,* 9.24.34, trans. A.C. Bhaktivedanta Swami Prabhupāda, http://srimadbhagavatam.com/9/24/en.
11. Tabor, *The Jesus Dynasty,* 60.

Let's pick up the story in the Gospel of Luke. We are told that Joseph took Mary to register for the official census in their ancestral town. For them, that was Bethlehem, about six miles south of Jerusalem, the town of David. Mary and Joseph were both descendants of King David, according to the genealogies in Matthew and Luke. Many others, it seems, were also coming to register, so many that the hotels were packed. Mary and Joseph ended up having to seek shelter in a rock grotto normally used to stable animals. That is the common Christian image of Christmas morning, the baby Jesus in a manger, warmed by the breath of an ox and an ass and visited by shepherds watching their flocks of sheep nearby. But it is only Luke who tells us about the manger and the shepherds. In a brilliant new book, Kenneth Bailey questions this traditional Christmas-card-like picture of the nativity. He argues that the images of the nativity in Middle Eastern Christian tradition are not the same as the Christmas-card images so familiar to Christians in the West. Bailey questions the likelihood that anyone from within Middle Eastern culture, or any culture for that matter, would turn away a pregnant woman on the verge of delivering her baby. Looking at the specific Greek words used in the original texts of Luke's gospel he suggests that the "inn" (*katalyma* in Greek in Luke's gospel) is the guest room in a private home rather than a commercial inn (which in Greek would be *pandocheion*). So, when Luke says that there was no room in the inn, he meant that the guest room was already occupied. Remember, many people were coming to Bethlehem to register, and most of them had relatives there. Since the guest room was already occupied, Mary and Joseph were invited to take shelter in the main room of the house. After the birth of the child, he was placed in a manger, a trough either stone or wood where animals were fed *in* the main family room. The shepherds who came to see the newborn baby would have recognized a domestic setting much like their own—a typical Middle Eastern peasant home.[12]

Matthew says that Jesus was visited by wise men, the "three kings" from the East who came to Palestine following a star. Kenneth Bailey makes a very convincing case that these wise men, possibly astrologers, came from Arabia. It is a well-established tradition in the Middle East that they brought gifts (gold, myrrh, and frankincense) that normally came to Palestine either from or through Arabia. In 1957, Bailey had a conversation with a British scholar, E.F.F. Bishop, who had visited a Muslim Bedouin tribe in Jordan called al-Kokabani. The word *kokab* means "planet"; *al-kokabani* means "those who study/follow planets." When Bishop asked why they were called that, they said that "their ancestors followed planets and traveled west to Palestine to

12. Kenneth Bailey, *Jesus through Middle Eastern Eyes* (Dovers Grove, IL: InterVarsity Press, 2008), 32–33.

show honor to the great prophet Jesus when he was born."[13] The al-Kokabani
are Arab Muslims.

> Here is what the Quran says of the actual birth of Jesus:
> And the pains of childbirth drove her to the trunk of a palm-tree:
>   she cried (in her anguish): "Ah! would that I had died
>   this! Would that I had been a thing forgotten and out
>   of sight!"
> But (a voice) cried to her from beneath the (palm-tree): "Grieve not!
>   for thy Lord hath provided a rivulet beneath thee;
> "And shake towards thyself the trunk of the palm-tree: it will let fall
>   fresh ripe dates upon thee.
> "So eat and drink and cool (thine) eye. And if thou dost see any man
>   say 'I have vowed a fast to (Allah) Most Gracious and this
>   day will I enter into no talk with any human being'"
>   (Quran 19:23–26).

Some Muslim exegetes identify the voice to be that of Gabriel. Others say
that it was Jesus in her womb.[14] Otherwise, Mary seems to be all alone, not
assisted by anyone. In Eastern Orthodox Christianity, she might have been
assisted by other women, but there would not have been any man present at
the birth itself.[15] A Coptic Orthodox scholar and monk offers this reflection:

> My heart goes out to this solitary mother.
> How did she endure labor pains alone?
> How did she receive her child with her own hands?
> How did she wrap him while her strength was totally exhausted?
> What did she have to eat or drink?
> O women of the world, witness this mother of the savior.
> How much did she suffer and how much does she deserve honor,
> …along with our tenderness and love?[16]

So, both Eastern Orthodox tradition and the Quran stress Mary's solitude.
    The Quran says that Mary gave birth to Jesus under a palm tree. This is
not a contradiction of what we read in the Gospel of Luke. Muslim tradition
accepts that the birth took place in Bethlehem and that she gave birth under
this palm tree. The Quran does not say what happened right after that, that
is, where she placed the child immediately after he was born. Quite possibly,
she might have moved the baby inside the cave/stable, or even into the family

13. Ibid., 52–53.
14. *Tafsir Ibn Kathir*, http://www.tafsir.com/default.asp?sid=19&tid=31153.
15. Bailey, *Jesus*, 34.
16. Matta al-Miskin, al-Injil, bi-Hasab Bisharat al-Qiddis Luqa (Cairo: Dayr al-Qiddis Anba
Maqar, 1998), 128 (cited in and translated by Bailey, *Jesus*, 34).

room of a private home as Bailey suggests, and placed him in a manger. Surely, we cannot imagine Mary actually giving birth in a manger (literally a feeding trough). But we can imagine her feeling the pains of childbirth! Verse 23 in the Quran provides an insight that appears neither in the Gospel of Matthew nor in the Gospel of Luke. The tone is not at all like in the Greek myths of Zeus fathering Apollo or Minos. Only in the Quran do we read of the pains of childbirth. How real can it get! Mary surely must have felt them. The Quran could not have copied this particular detail from the gospel accounts. In fact, a Muslim woman recently pointed out to me that, for her, this was confirmation that the Quran was the inspired words of God. "A man would never have thought of that," she said. In the Quran, like in the Bible, we get the sense in all three birth narratives that this is the story of real people in real time.

The date palm is a very important element in Muslim tradition. In this case, it underscores God's nurturing of Mary, his having chosen her for the special task of giving birth to Jesus. This is the second time that God provided for Mary in a very special way. Quran 3:37 says:

> Right graciously did her Lord accept her: He made her grow in purity and beauty; to the care of Zakariya was she assigned. Every time that he entered (her) chamber to see her he found her supplied with sustenance. He said: "O Mary! whence (comes) this to you?" She said: "From Allah: for Allah provides sustenance to whom He pleases without measure."

In this first instance, the sustenance comes without Mary having to do anything. Incidentally, this same story is told in in the *Protoevangelium* of James, 8.[17] In the second instance, under the palm tree, Mary participates in the miracle by having to shake the palm tree.

This reminds me of a late fifteenth-century Christmas carol, "the Cherry Tree Carol," where, as the story goes, Mary and Joseph are on their way to Bethlehem to register for the census. They pass through a cherry orchard, and Mary asks Joseph for some cherries. He answers: "Let him pluck thee some cherries that got thee with child." Then, the babe in Mary's womb spoke: "Bow down, good cherry tree, to my mother's hand." The cherry tree complied. The ballad is actually based on a variant of that story in one of the non-canonical gospels, the Pseudo Gospel of Matthew;[18] and in this case, it is not a cherry tree but a palm tree as in the Quran. In that gospel, the holy family—Mary, Joseph, and Jesus—has just left for Egypt, fleeing Herod's

17. http://www.newadvent.org/fathers/0847.htm.
18. http://www.gnosis.org/library/psudomat.htm.

persecution. It was on the third day into the journey that the holy family passed through a palm grove. Mary said to Joseph how wonderful it would be if they could reach for some of the dates high up in the tree, apparently out of reach. Jesus commanded the tree to lower its branches so they could reach the dates. The palm tree did.

Getting back to the issue of the virgin birth, if Luke is correct in verse 2:5 that Mary and Joseph were only engaged when they went to Bethlehem, then the couple were still not married. There is the issue of the birth of a child out of wedlock. Commenting on Quran verses 19:27–28: "At length she brought the (babe) to her people carrying him (in her arms). They said: 'O Mary! Truly an amazing thing hast thou brought! O sister of Aaron! thy father was not a man of evil nor thy mother a woman unchaste!'" Quran translator Abdallah Yusuf Ali says: "The amazement of the people knew no bounds. In any case they were ready to think the worst of her, as she had disappeared from her kin for some time. But now she comes, shamelessly parading a babe in her arms! How she had disgraced the house of Aaron, the fountain of priesthood!" Soon the people would know that this was no ordinary birth of no ordinary child. The story continues:

> But she pointed to the babe. They said: "How can we talk to one
>   who is a child in the cradle?"
> He said: "I am indeed a servant of God: he hath given me revelation
>   and made me a prophet;
> "And he hath made me blessed wheresoever I be and hath enjoined
>   on me prayer and charity as long as I live;
> "(He) hath made me kind to my mother and not overbearing or
>   miserable" (Quran 19:29–32).

Yes, in the Quranic version, Jesus speaks as a newborn infant. And so he does in the Cherry Tree Carol. That would not be possible if he were an ordinary child, but he was not—not in the Bible and not in the Quran. Listen to what he says, especially in verse 33: "So Peace is on me the day I was born the day that I die and the Day that I shall be raised up to life (again)"! A reference to this event we have just witnessed, to be sure, but also a reference to his death, ascension, and second coming on the day of judgment, that we will take up in a later chapter.

The gospels tell us very little about Jesus' childhood. There is really only one story in the Gospel of Luke 2:41–52 about Jesus going to Jerusalem with his parents for the Feast of Passover. He was twelve years old. After the feast was over, his parents left for the journey home, but Jesus stayed behind in Jerusalem. Mary and Joseph did not notice that he was missing until the end of the day, assuming that he was traveling with some other relatives. They rushed back to Jerusalem and found Jesus only on the third day, sitting among the scholars in the temple courts listening and asking questions. We don't know what they talked about, but Luke tells us that "everyone was amazed at his understanding and his answers" (Luke 2:47). I get the sense somehow that Jesus got the best of them in intellectual discourse, as he did so many times during the three years of his public life as an adult. There is no mention of this event in the Quran, or anywhere else in Muslim tradition. But there are any number of stories in Muslim tradition that portray Jesus' rebuke of the *ulama*, the Muslim equivalent of the Scribes and Pharisees among the Jews of Jesus' time. One of my favorite stories goes like this:

> Christ said, "The most hateful of scholars to God is one who is fond of backbiting, who likes to occupy a seat of honor in an assembly, to be invited to feasts, and to have sacks of food emptied for him. Truly I say to you, such men have obtained their wages in this world, and God shall multiply their punishment on the Day of Judgment.[19]

It sounds a lot like what Jesus says in Matthew's gospel: "Everything they do is done for men to see: They make their phylacteries wide and the tassels on their garments long; they love the place of honor at banquets and the most important seats in the synagogues; they love to be greeted in the marketplaces and to have men call them 'Rabbi'"(Matthew 23:5–7, NIV).

We also get the sense that Jesus was a troublesome child for Mary and Joseph. He could have told them that he had business in the temple. He must have known that he would cause them great distress by his absence for three days. And indeed he did! When they scolded him, his only defense was that he was about doing his father's business—a defense that Christians readily accept. Luke goes on to say that they all returned to Nazareth and (from then on) he "was obedient to them. But his mother treasured all these things in her heart. And Jesus grew in wisdom and stature, and in favor with God and men" (Luke 2:51–52, NIV).

The canonical gospels are totally silent about Jesus' life before this encounter with the teachers in the temple. We know almost nothing of his early childhood from the gospels.[20] There is, on the other hand, an early second-century body of literature known as the Infancy Gospels which provides some detail. The earliest of these is the Infancy Gospel of Thomas. Judas Thomas was thought by some early Christians to have been the author and Jesus' own

19. Abdallah ibn Qutayba (d. 884), `Uyun, quoted in Tarif Khalidi, *The Muslim Jesus* (Cambridge, MA and London: Harvard University Press, 2001), 103.
20. Bart D. Ehrman, *Lost Scriptures: Books that Did Not Make It into the New Testament* (New York: Oxford University Press, 2003), 57–62.

brother. Some scholars, and at least one popular writer,[21] claim that Jesus spent his early growing up years in Egypt. We do know that when he was still an infant, his parents took him to Egypt. The Gospel of Matthew tells us that Herod was out to kill Jesus. An angel of the Lord appeared to Joseph in a dream and told him to take his family to Egypt. So Joseph took Mary and their newborn baby across the Sinai to the land of the Nile. Matthew also tells us that they returned to Galilee after Herod died; the date of his death is 4 BC. What we don't know is exactly how long after Herod died. If they returned soon after Herod's death, Jesus would have been one or two years old at the most. But Matthew is not specific about this particular point. He does stress that the sojourn into Egypt is to fulfill what is said through the prophet, "Out of Egypt I called my son" (Hosea 11:1).

The story in the Infancy Gospel begins when Jesus was five years old. It quickly confirms that Jesus was no ordinary child—that he was somewhat of a mischievous child at best. One day when Jesus was walking through the village, another child ran past and bumped him in the shoulder. Jesus became angry and shouted at him, "you will go no further on your way!" And the child fell dead. Under pressure from the dead child's father and from his own father, Joseph, Jesus brought the child back to life. [22] This was one of several cures or resurrections that this "gospel" reports. On another occasion, Jesus was learning his letters with his tutor Zacheus. The teacher was introducing the letter Alpha. Jesus interrupted him and said, "Since you do not know the true nature of the Alpha, how can you teach anyone the Beta? You hypocrite!" And Jesus proceeded to lay out all of the set patterns of the letter Alpha,[23] displaying at the same time both precocious brilliance and contempt for pedantic scholars.

No one questions that Joseph continued to work as a carpenter as Jesus was growing up. We can assume that Jesus worked with Joseph as a carpenter's apprentice. In one of the stories in the Infancy Gospel of Thomas, Joseph was cutting lengths of wood for crossbeams. But he made a serious mistake and one of the beams was considerably too short. They were out of wood, and Joseph did not know what to do. Jesus told him to lay the shorter crossbeam next to a full length one. Jesus stretched the short one to the length of the longer one. The problem was solved.[24]

When Jesus was six years old, he went to the well to fetch water. He was jostled by the crowd and somehow broke the water jug. So, he gathered the

21. Anne Rice, *Christ the Lord Out of Egypt* (New York and Toronto: Alfred A. Knopf, 2005).
22. Ehrman, *Lost Scriptures*, 58.
23. Greek letters were introduced into mathematics long ago to provide a collection of useful symbols to stand for abstract objects, such as numbers, sets, functions, and spaces. See http://www.ndt-ed.org/GeneralResources/GreekLetters/GreekLetters.htm.
24. Ehrman, *Lost Scriptures*, 60.

water up and brought it home in his cloak. When he was eight years old, he was sowing grain with his father. Jesus sowed just one grain of wheat. By harvest time, that one grain had produced a hundred large bushels, enough for Jesus to feed to all of the poor and for Joseph to have plenty left.[25]

The most interesting to me of all stories of Jesus' miracles as a child took place at the ford of a stream. Jesus gathered the water into pools and made them immediately pure, simply by ordering the water to be pure. He then mixed some dirt with the water and fashioned twelve sparrows out of mud. Jesus was criticized for doing this because it was the Sabbath. When Joseph came to scold him, Jesus clapped his hands and ordered the birds to fly away. They did![26] None of these stories from the Infancy Gospel of Thomas are in the Bible. They are not in the Quran either, except for this one about making birds out of mud and breathing life into them. We will revisit this story again in the next chapter as we investigate the public life of Jesus, his miracles, and servanthood. The Infancy Gospel of Thomas did not make the final cut in the canon of the Bible, but it is clear that its stories were widely told in early Christian times, and people back then could marvel at the fanciful child Jesus. Today, the Coptic Church has a whole pilgrimage route in Egypt based on the time the holy family lived there, including the sites of some of these miracles.

Although there would be disagreement in early church councils about the nature of Mary's child, all of the early Christian creeds endorse the source of Mary's pregnancy, reflecting that it was generally accepted by the early Christian community. We have already discussed the historicity of the synoptic gospels. Matthew and Luke, although they provided different details about the birth, are in total agreement about the source of Mary's pregnancy. Although they cannot prove a virgin birth of Jesus, they have convinced mainstream Christians and Muslims alike.

Where Christians and Muslims will disagree on the virgin birth is why the concept is so important. For Muslims, the virgin birth is testimony to God's infinite creative power. God can, and in this case did, create by a sheer act of will. He said, "Be," and so it was. This was in fact the second time, according to the Quran, that God created a man by a simple act of his will. The first time was when he created Adam—without the intervention of a father or mother. It was simply an act of God's creative will. Additionally for Muslims, the purity of Mary is of the highest importance. Since Jesus was a prophet unlike the others, the purity of his mother needed to be established.

Adam, being the "first human," could not have come into the world with

25. Ibid.
26. Ibid., 58.

two biological parents. Jesus, on the other hand, assuming that God can do whatever He wants, could have, if God had wanted to do it that way. But He didn't. God *chose* to bring Jesus into the world through His own command *and* a biological mother. This distinguishes Jesus from Adam; it makes him special, unique. For Christians, that Jesus was "conceived by the Holy Spirit and born of the Virgin Mary" unites the divinity and the humanity of Jesus more clearly than any other way that Jesus could have come into the world. For Christians, the virgin birth has an added significance. It speaks to the question of whether or not Jesus is the Son of God—whether or not, indeed, Jesus is God—a question that, too, will have to be taken up again in our discussion of the trinity.

CHAPTER FOUR

Jesus the Perfect Servant

Here is my servant whom I have chosen, the one I love... (Matthew 12:18, NIV)

Say Like this. If anyone wonders how Jesus raised the dead,
Don't try to explain the miracle.
Kiss me on the lips.
Like this. Like this.[1]

MIRACLE WORKER

Performing miracles can be dangerous work. Jesus knew this, so he warned those who saw him cure the sick not to tell anyone.[2] He had just withdrawn from the view of the Pharisees who were out to get him for curing the sick on the Sabbath. It is in this context that the author of the Gospel of Matthew refers back to the book of Isaiah and identifies Jesus as the servant of the Lord, "my servant whom I have chosen, the one I love..." (Matthew 12:14–18).

Jesus performed dozens of healing miracles. He made it so the deaf could hear, the mute could speak, the blind could see, the lame could walk. He cured lepers. He freed people who were possessed of demons. He raised people from the dead. And he restored a soldier's ear that had been cut off by one of his disciples. Most of Jesus' miracles are told in all three of the synoptic gospels, the Gospels of Matthew, Mark, and Luke. The Gospel of Mark is the earliest of the three, written, we think, sometime between the years 65 and 70. New Testament scholars believe that it is likely that Matthew and Luke, both written from ten to twenty years later, got a lot of their material from Mark. A couple of miracles mentioned in Mark, the healing of the blind man at Bethsaida and the healing of the blind man Bartemaius, were not picked

1. http://www.shamsitabriz.net/shamsandrumimevlana.html.
2. There were several reasons why Jesus avoided publicizing his miracles. Matthew 12:16 and 16:20 express concern for repercussions from the Pharisees and Roman authorities. The time for Jesus' arrest had not yet come.

up by either Matthew or Luke. They do mention such cures in general, but it seems that they just left out the specific names. Luke is the only one of the three to mention the restoring of the soldier's severed ear. Though Mark seems to be the source for much of their material, they must have had another source as well. Some scholars refer to this other source as Q, a source other than Mark from which both Matthew and Luke drew material. There were likely other sources, too—from which only Matthew drew, and from which only Luke drew—hence their singular reporting of certain incidents in Jesus' life. Then there is the Gospel of John. He reports none of the miracles told in the synoptic gospels, but, alone, tells of four others: the healing of an official's son, the healing of a crippled man by the Pool of Bethesda, the healing of a man who was born blind, and the raising of Lazarus from the dead. The Gospel of John seems to be drawing on sources completely different from the synoptic gospels. That has to be a good thing. Different reporters pick up different details, not contradictory, but rather complementary.

Jesus performed other kinds of miracles—miracles that we could call "nature miracles"—in which he altered or defied the normal course of nature. He calmed a violent storm (Matthew 8:23–27, Mark 4:36–41, Luke 8:22–25); he walked on water (Matthew 14:22–23, Mark 6:45–51); he allowed Peter to walk on water as long as his faith held him afloat (Matthew 14:29–30). The Quran does not specifically mention these nature miracles. But Islamic tradition does. Here is a relevant *hadith* reported by Ahmad Ibn Hanbal:

> The Disciples failed to find their prophet, so they went out to seek him and found him walking upon water. One of them said to him, "Prophet of God, shall we walk toward you?" "Yes," he replied. As the disciple put one foot forward and then the next, he sank. Jesus said, "Stretch forth your hand, you man of little faith. If the son of Adam had a grain or atom's weight of faith, he would walk upon water."[3]

The very first miracle in his "public" life was one of these nature miracles. We read about it in the Gospel of John (2:1–11). Jesus and his disciples had been invited to a wedding in the town of Cana in Galilee. Jesus' mother was there too, and she became concerned when the host embarrassingly ran out of wine to serve his guests. She came to Jesus to see if he could solve the problem, a suggestion that she must have seen him do this sort of thing before. At first he was annoyed with Mary, but in the end he did change water into wine; we are not talking about just a few bottles of wine here; we are talking about six

3. Ahmad Ibn Hanbal, *Kitab al-Zuhd*, cited in Tarif Khalidi, *The Muslim Jesus: Sayings and Stories in Islamic Literature* (Cambridge, MA and London: Harvard University Press, 2001), 73.

huge vats of water into wine. The practice was to serve the best wine first and then to serve poorer wine when guests' taste was less discriminating. But this time, the wine that the guests were served last, the wine that Jesus made, was the best of all.

Jesus was obviously sensitive to the thirst and hunger of others. Remember the story from the Infancy Gospel that we saw in the previous chapter, the story about the child Jesus expanding the wheat harvest to provide for the community in abundance. That story does not show up in the canonical gospels, but we do see Jesus there as an adult feeding multitudes. All four of the canonical gospels tell the story of Jesus feeding a crowd of five thousand men with only five loaves of bread and two fishes. All four are perfectly consistent about the number of loaves and fishes, and they all agree that there were twelve full baskets of food left over after everyone was fed. Only John mentions that it was a small boy who supplied the bread and the two fishes. Mark and Luke provide the number of five thousand men. Matthew adds that that number did not include women and children. Luke is the only one who tells the name of the town where this took place. Matthew and Mark tell another story in which Jesus, at a later time, fed a crowd of four thousand people. This time, there were seven baskets of food left.

The point here is that Jesus fed people when they were hungry, and there was food in abundance. The Quran tells us this as well in the chapter called *Al-Ma'idah*, "The Table":

> Behold! the disciples said: "O Jesus the son of Mary! can thy Lord send down to us a table set (with viands) from heaven?" Said Jesus: "Fear God if ye have faith."
> They said: "We only wish to eat thereof and satisfy our hearts and to know that thou hast indeed told us the truth; and that we ourselves may be witnesses to the miracle."
> Said Jesus the son of Mary: "O God our Lord! send us from heaven a table set (with viands) that there may be for us for the first and the last of us a solemn festival and a sign from Thee; and provide for our sustenance for Thou art the best Sustainer (of our needs)" (Quran 5:112–114).

Of these verses, Abdallah Yusuf Ali's commentary says this:

> Even in the Canonical Gospels, so many of the miracles are concerned with food and drink, e.g., the turning of the water into wine (John 2:1–11); the conversion of five loaves and two small fishes into food for 5,000 men (John 5:5–13), this being the only miracle recorded in all the four Gospels; the miraculous number of fishes caught for food (Luke 5:4–11); the cursing of the fig tree because it had no

fruit (Matthew 21:18–19); the allegory of eating Christ's flesh and drinking his blood (John 6:53–57).

This last point is a reference to the Last Supper. It was the Thursday night before the Friday of the crucifixion. Jesus had gathered in an upper room with his disciples to share a Passover meal. The literal act of breaking bread together is, perhaps, a much more powerful bonding force in Middle Eastern culture than it is in the West. During the meal, Jesus took a loaf of bread; he gave thanks, broke the bread into pieces and gave some to each of his disciples saying, "take and eat; this is my body." Then he took a cup of wine and again gave thanks and offered it to them saying, "Drink from it all of you. This is my blood..." (Matthew 26:26–31, Mark 14:22–24, Luke 22:19–20). Christians commemorate this event with the sacrament of communion. Most Christians believe that in communion Jesus is somehow sacramentally, miraculously, mysteriously, and mystically present. A number of Muslim scholars see a connection between this Last Supper and the table that God sent from heaven as described in Quran 5:112–114. In both cases, the allegory, the mythical truth if you will, has to do with Jesus providing spiritual nourishment to his followers who are hungry to know the truth about God. Our "chain-linked Bible–Quran" might have linked Quran 5:112–114 to Psalm 23:5, "You prepare a table before me," or to John 6:33, "For the bread of God is that which comes down out of heaven, and gives life to the world."

Jesus' miracles are pretty well cross referenced in the canonical gospels, albeit different gospels in some cases providing different details, again not contradicting details but rather complementary. The Quran does not have much to add. In fact, by the time the Quran is revealed, there seems to be no need to retell all of these miracle stories over again in great detail. Rather, about all of the miracles the Quran just makes a broad, general statement. Just a few verses before Jesus talked about feeding his hungry disciples, God said:

> O Jesus the son of Mary! recount my favor to thee and to thy mother. Behold! I strengthened thee with the holy spirit so that thou didst speak to the people in childhood and in maturity. Behold! I taught thee the Book and Wisdom the Law and the Gospel. And behold! thou makest out of clay as it were the figure of a bird *by my leave* [emphasis added] and thou breathest into it and it becometh a bird *by my leave* [emphasis added] and thou healest those born blind and the lepers *by my leave* [emphasis added]. And behold! thou bringest forth the dead *by my leave* [emphasis added] (Quran 5:110).

The Quran does list one miracle that does not appear in the canonical gospels nor anywhere else in the New Testament. It is the making of birds out of clay, breathing life into them and watching them fly off as living creatures. The Quran is not the first to tell this particular story. We have already seen it in the Infancy Gospel of Thomas described in the chapter on Jesus' birth and childhood. The Quran does not say anything about any of the other stories from the Infancy Gospels. So, why this particular one? It could be because it says something special about Jesus, something that sets him apart from all of the other of God's messengers mentioned in the Quran, even the prophet Muhammad.

There are certain things that Muslims will not say about Jesus. No Muslim would say that "Jesus is God." As a categorical statement of "truth," that would contradict what most Christians believe. But the issue of relationship between divinity and humanity in the person of Jesus is more complicated than a simple truth statement, and we will return to this question in the chapter on the trinity. For now, at the very least, the story of Jesus making birds out of clay and giving them life by breathing life into them asks Muslims to believe that Jesus facilitated life in God's name, or with God's permission. The important point to notice here is that the rhetoric of Jesus breathing life into birds of clay is virtually identical to the rhetoric of God breathing life into man. Link to Quran 15:28–29, "Behold! thy Lord said to the angels: 'I am about to create man from sounding clay from mud molded into shape; when I have fashioned him (in due proportion) and breathed into him of my spirit, fall ye down in obeisance unto him." God created man out of clay and breathed his own spirit into him. The famous Muslim mystic Ibn al-'Arabi explains this exceptional role of Jesus this way: "God reserved for Jesus to be the Spirit, and accorded him, to the exclusion of all that He created from clay, the supplemental gift of life giving breath. God, Who reserved this power for Himself, gave it to no person other than Jesus."[4]

Christians believe that Jesus as *Logos* was there and participated in the act of creation as it is described in the Book of Genesis. God created through the power of his word. "And God said, 'Let there be light,' and there was light" (Genesis 1:3). The opening lines of the Gospel of John identify Jesus as being that creative force, that is, the Word of God.

When the Quran says that Jesus performed miracles "by my (God's) leave," what exactly did God mean when he said "by my leave"? Abdallah Yusuf Ali, in his note to Quran 5:110 says that the words "are repeated with each miracle to emphasize the fact that they arose, not out of the power or will of Jesus, but by the leave and will and power of God, who is supreme

4. Cited from Faouzi Skali, *Jésus dans la tradition soufie* (Paris: Editions Albin Michel, 2004), 91, translation mine.

over Jesus as He is over all other mortals." Is the "power" of Jesus the same thing as the "will" of Jesus? One of the overriding themes of the gospels seems to be submission to the will of God. Here is where the New Testament might shed some light on the phrase "by my leave." A recent article in the magazine *Muslim Sunrise*[5] says that there are three hundred references in the New Testament to Jesus subordinating himself to the will of God. Jesus made this very clear when he was teaching people how to pray. "Your kingdom come, Your will be done, on earth as it is in heaven," Jesus taught. (Matthew 6:10). And he set himself as the example in the very dramatic scene in the Garden of Gethsemane, sweating drops of blood, he said: "Father, if you are willing, remove this cup from me; yet not my will, but Yours be done" (Luke 22:42).

People were always trying to nail Jesus down. They wanted to know just what or who he was or claimed or claimed not to be. They tried to catch him in some kind of misstatement like advocating withholding one's taxes from the Roman occupation government, or in some kind of misdeed, like doing something that was forbidden on the Sabbath. There is a theme that runs through his responses to their questions and criticisms. Jesus said to them, "Truly, truly, I say to you, the Son can do nothing of Himself, unless *it is* something He sees the Father doing...." (John 5:19). A few verses later he said, "I can do nothing on my own initiative. As I hear, I judge; and my judgment is just, because I do not seek my own will, but the will of Him who sent me" (John 5:30). And still further, "I do nothing on my own initiative, but I speak these things as the Father taught me" (John 8:28). Of his miracles, Jesus specifically said, "The miracles I do in my Father's name speak for me" (John 10:25, NIV). The apostles, too, saw Jesus' miracles as the work of God. The writer of Acts says: "Men of Israel, listen to this: Jesus of Nazareth was a man accredited by God to you by miracles, wonders and signs, which God did among you through him, as you yourselves know" (Acts: 2:22, NIV). *Miracles...signs, which God did among you through Jesus.* Jesus performed miracles as a sign of God's power. Our chain-linked Bible–Quran at this point refers us to Quran 43:61: "When Jesus came with Clear Signs he said: 'Now have I come to you with Wisdom and in order to make clear to you some of the (points) on which ye dispute: therefore fear God and obey me.'"

TEACHER

Jesus came with clear signs. He came so that humankind could know God, learn about God. Among everything else that Jesus might have been, he was a teacher. On the northern shore of the Sea of Galilee, on a hillside that

---

5. J. D. Shams, "Jesus: God or Beloved of God?" *Muslim Sunrise*, Spring 2006, 12–18.

became known as the Mount of Beatitudes, Jesus held what is perhaps his most famous class:

> Now when he saw the crowds, he went up on a mountainside and sat down.
> His disciples came to him, and he began to teach them, saying:
> Blessed are the poor in spirit, for theirs is the kingdom of heaven.
> Blessed are those who mourn, for they will be comforted.
> Blessed are the meek, for they will inherit the earth.
> Blessed are those who hunger and thirst for righteousness, for they will be filled.
> Blessed are the merciful, for they will be shown mercy.
> Blessed are the pure in heart, for they will see God.
> Blessed are the peacemakers, for they will be called sons of God.
> Blessed are those who are persecuted because of righteousness,
> for theirs is the kingdom of heaven.
> Blessed are you when people insult you, persecute you and falsely say all kinds of evil against you because of me (Matthew 5:1–11, NIV).

The phrase "blessed are..." reflects not only Jesus' style of speaking, but also a dominant theme in his teaching, a style and theme that is captured in so many sayings that are attributed to Jesus in Muslim tradition (*hadith*). Typical is the *hadith* reported by Abu'l-Hassan al-Amiri (d. 992). "Jesus said, 'The merciful in this world is the one who will be shown mercy in the next world.'"[6] Jesus reminded his listeners of the importance of forgiving as well as being forgiven when he taught them how to pray (Matthew 6:12), and when he told Peter to forgive his brother seventy times seven (Matthew 18:22). The Quran reminds the faithful at the beginning of every chapter that God is all merciful.

Jesus was an itinerant teacher, and he asked his disciples to be itinerants as well. He urged them to be like the birds and to depend on God to provide the resources they would need to do what God called them to do (Matthew 6:25–27). Abdallah ibn al-Mubarak gives us this *hadith*:

> Jesus said: "Strive for the sake of God and not for the sake of your bellies, Look at the birds coming and going! They neither reap nor plow, and God provides for them. If you say, 'Our bellies are larger than the bellies of birds,' then look at these cattle, wild or tame, as they come and go, neither reaping nor plowing, and God provides for them too. Beware the excesses of the world, for the excesses of the world are an abomination in God's eyes."[7]

"Take mosques to be your homes, houses to be stopping places. Eat from

6. Abu'l-Hasan al-Amiri, *Al-Sa'ada wa'l-Is'ad*, cited in Khalidi, *The Muslim Jesus*, 138.
7. Abdallah ibn al-Mubarak, *Kitab al-Zuhd*, cited in Khalidi, *The Muslim Jesus*, 60.

the plants of the wilderness and escape from this world in peace," said Jesus according to Muslim tradition.[8] There is a Muslim prayer that says: "Wandering like a pilgrim belongs to the prophet of God, Isa" (Isa is the Arabic name for Jesus).[9]

After Jesus recited a list of beatitudes, he proceeded to teach what it would mean to be a righteous person. He reminded his listeners to obey the commandments. "Do not murder" (Matthew 5:21, NIV); "Do not commit adultery" (Matthew 5:27, NIV). We often think of Islam as being especially hard on adulterers, stoning them to death. But Jesus was pretty hard on adulterers too. He said that if we were tempted to commit adultery, we should consider tearing out our eye which would be better than losing one's soul (Matthew 5:29). The famous medieval Muslim scholar al-Ghazzali (d.1111) tells this story about Jesus:

> It is told that Jesus went out one day to pray for rain. When those around him became restless, Jesus said, "Whoever among you who has committed a sin must return." So they all went back, except for one man who stayed behind with him in the desert. Jesus said to him, "Have you not committed any sins?" "As God is my witness," he answered, "none that I know of. Except that one day, while I was praying, a woman passed near me and I looked at her with this eye. As she passed by, I put my finger into my eye and plucked it out, and flung it at the woman." Then Jesus said to him, "Pray to God so that I may call 'Amen' to your prayer." The man prayed to God, the sky became covered with clouds, and it poured. And so they were quenched.[10]

The Quran is more lenient than Muslim tradition and practice that evolved over time. The Quran says to punish adulterers, both men and women, by a hundred lashes, and that only if four eye witnesses can be brought forth to testify to the adulterous act (Quran 24:2–4). On the other hand, God's mercy is prepared to soften the harshness of the law. Just as Jesus was able to forgive the adulteress whose faith and repentance were sincere, so too, the Quran says that God will do the same:

> O Prophet! when believing women come to thee to take the oath of fealty to thee that they will not associate in worship any other thing whatever with God, that they will not steal that they will not commit adultery...and that they will not disobey thee in any just matter, then do thou receive their fealty and pray to God for the forgiveness (of their sins): for God is Oft-Forgiving Most Merciful (Quran 60:12).

8. Ibid., 58.
9. Constance Padwick, *Muslim Devotions*, 1961, 168, cited in Parrinder, *Jesus in the Qur'an*, 40.
10. Abu Hamid al-Ghazzali, *Ihya' 'Ulum al-Din*, cited in Khalidi, *The Muslim Jesus*, 167.

Jesus assured his listeners that he was not here to abolish the laws that were revealed to them in the Old Testament. Far from it. He was here to fill the commandments up with meaning by revealing the will of God that stands behind the letter of the Old Testament commandments. To be righteous would mean to go beyond what it says in the law. Jesus said essentially the same thing in the Quran: "(I have come to you) to attest the Law which was before me and to make lawful to you part of what was (before) forbidden to you; I have come to you with a Sign from your Lord" (Quran 3:50).

What Jesus is talking about here is a relationship between God and humankind, a relationship based on love. Jesus was talking about a commandment greater than all of the other commandments. People asked him point blank: "Teacher, which is the greatest commandment in the Law?" Jesus replied: "Love the Lord your God with all your heart and with all your soul and with all your mind. This is the first and greatest commandment. And the second is like it: Love your neighbor as yourself. All the Law and the Prophets hang on these two commandments" (Matthew 22:36–40, NIV). The Pharisees were hoping to catch Jesus off guard with this question, but in fact he was quoting from the scripture that they professed; he was quoting from the Book of Leviticus 19:18. The spirit of the law had been there all along.

This greatest of commandments is also a cornerstone in Islam. It is one of the seven conditions for the *Shahadah*, the profession of faith. Without love, the profession of faith, "there is no God but God," is meaningless. This condition is established in the Quran: "... it is righteousness to believe in God and the Last Day, and the Angels, and the Book and the Messengers; to spend of your substance, out of love for Him, for your kin, for orphans, for the needy, for the wayfarer, for those who ask, and for the ransom of slaves" (Quran 2:177). "And hold fast, all together, by the rope which God (stretches out for you), and be not divided among yourselves; and remember with gratitude God's favor on you; for you were enemies and He joined your hearts in love, so that by His grace you became brethren"(Quran 3:103). Abdallah Yusuf Ali's note to Quran 2:177: "we are given a beautiful description of the righteous and God-fearing man. He should obey salutary regulation, but he should fix his gaze on the love of God and the love of his fellow-men." Muslims have believed this for a long time. An early *hadith* says:

> A man came to Jesus and said, "Teacher of goodness, teach me something that you know and I do not...How can a servant be truly pious before God?" Jesus replied, "You must truly love God in your heart and work in his service, exerting all your effort and strength,

and be merciful toward the people of your race as you show mercy to yourself." He said, "Teacher of goodness, who are the people of my race?" Jesus replied, "All the children of Adam. And that which you do not wish done to you, do not do to others. In this way you will be truly pious before god."[11]

THE PERFECT SERVANT

Ever wonder what Jesus looked like? The earliest painting that we have that might be Jesus is in a small house/church in the city of Dura Europas, in modern-day Syria; it dates from the third century. It looks nothing like the portraits imagined by Renaissance artists. Which is correct? The New Testament will be of little help here since it provides not a single description of his physical appearance. Neither does the Quran, but Islamic tradition going all the way back to the prophet Muhammad does provide a description. How would Muhammad know what Jesus looked like? Jesus was among the prophets Muhammad met on his famous night journey from Mecca to Jerusalem and from there to meet face to face with God. Was this a literal physical journey as most Muslims believe, or was it a spiritual journey through a metaphorical vision? Either way, Muhammad did have some kind of special encounter with God. The Quran does tell us that the night journey occurred but does not provide any details of the encounter itself. We have to depend on Muslim tradition for that. *Hadith*s that describe the night journey, based on what Muhammad told people about it after the fact, marvel at the fact that within just a few hours time, so the story goes, Muhammad was able to give a detailed description of Jerusalem without ever having been there before. *Hadith*s also tell of conversations that Muhammad had with prophets along the way. And among those he met was Jesus. Muhammad left us with this description of what he looked like. Jesus was a broad-chested man of medium height, and medium build. He had short, curly hair and had a reddish complexion, "as if he had just come out from a hot bath."[12] Except for the broad-chested part, this seems to be describing the portrait at Dura Europas. Is it accurate? Hard to tell. But it's still nice to have a concrete image in mind.

When God said of Jesus: "Here is my servant whom I have chosen, the one I love; in whom I delight; I will put my Spirit on him..." (Matthew 12:18, NIV) he echoed what was revealed in the Book of Isaiah 42:1, the first of a series of servant-of-the-Lord oracles that runs through the next twelve chapters. Who the servant was to Second Isaiah is not entirely clear. At times the servant seems to be an individual, that is, a prophet; at other times, the

---

11. Ahmad Ibn Hanbal, *Kitab al-Zuhd*, cited in Khalidi, *The Muslim Jesus*, 79.
12. Sahih al-Bukhari, *Hadith* 4.608 and 4.648, cited in *Alim*, Islamic Software.

text identifies the servant as the nation of Israel. By the time the gospels were written, the Gospel of Matthew clearly associates the servant in the Book of Isaiah with Jesus Christ. At the time that Isaiah was written, its readers could not have done that.

Remember my conversation with our host at the Journalists and Writers Foundation in Istanbul, when I asked how the Gülen movement preached tolerance and love for the "other"? "Through example and humility, just like when Jesus washed the feet of his disciples." That is the classic image of Jesus as the perfect servant—the scene at the Last Supper when Jesus washes the feet of his disciples (John 13:5ff.). We are taught that in Biblical times, it was the custom for servants to wash the feet of the master or the master's guests when they came in from the dusty road and removed their sandals. The very act of washing someone's feet is not only an act of service, but also an act of humility. Peter was so turned off by the idea of Jesus humiliating himself by washing his feet that he said, "You shall never wash my feet." When Jesus rebuked him, Peter changed his mind: "Then, Lord...not just my feet but my hands and my head as well!" John 13:8–9, NIV). In Muslim tradition, Jesus washed the hands of his disciples as they sat down together for the Passover meal.[13] It is still the custom in the Islamic world today for the host to wash the guests' hands when they sit down to share a meal. It is a sign of the perfect servant.

In the Quran, Jesus identified himself as God's servant: "I am indeed a servant of God, he said." (Quran 19:30). Quran 4:172 says: "Christ disdaineth not to serve and worship God." The Arabic word for servant here is *abd*. In this context, it has no connotation of a demeaning status. Quite on the contrary, it means complete submission to and worship of God. Any Muslim would be proud to be called a servant of God, and indeed, many Muslim parents name their male children Abd Allah, servant of God. Abdallah Yusuf Ali comments on Quran 4:172: "Christ often watched and prayed, as a humble worshipper of God; and his agony in the Garden of Gethsemane was full of human dignity, suffering, and self-humiliation."

By the end of the series of the servant-of-the-Lord oracles in Isaiah, the servant has become a suffering servant:

> He was despised and rejected by men, a man of sorrows, and familiar with suffering.
> Like one from whom men hide their faces he was despised, and we esteemed him not.

13. Benjamin Todd Lawson, "The Crucifixion in the Qur'an and Qur'anic commentary: A Historical Survey," *The Bulletin of the Henry Martyn Institute of Islamic Studies* 10, issue 2 (Hyderbad, India, 1991): 45–46.

Surely he took up our infirmities and carried our sorrows, yet we considered him stricken by God, smitten by him, and afflicted.

But he was pierced for our transgressions, he was crushed for our iniquities; the punishment that brought us peace was upon him, and by his wounds we are healed.

We all, like sheep, have gone astray, each of us has turned to his own way; and the Lord has laid on him the iniquity of us all.

He was oppressed and afflicted, yet he did not open his mouth; he was led like a lamb to the slaughter, and as a sheep before her shearers is silent, so he did not open his mouth.

By oppression and judgment he was taken away. And who can speak of his descendants?

For he was cut off from the land of the living; for the transgression of my people he was stricken.

He was assigned a grave with the wicked, and with the rich in his death, though he had done no violence, nor was any deceit in his mouth.

Yet it was the Lord's will to crush him and cause him to suffer, and though the Lord makes his life a guilt offering, he will see his offspring and prolong his days, and the will of the Lord will prosper in his hand.

After the suffering of his soul, he will see the light of life and be satisfied; by his knowledge my righteous servant will justify many, and he will bear their iniquities.

Therefore I will give him a portion among the great, and he will divide the spoils with the strong, because he poured out his life unto death, and was numbered with the transgressors. For he bore the sin of many, and made intercession for the transgressors (Isaiah 53:3–12, NIV).

Jesus saw his own servanthood as one of a suffering servant. He told his followers that in the Gospel of Matthew. He said: "For even the Son of man did not come to be served, but to serve, and to give his life as a ransom for many" (Mark 10:45). Christians and Muslims alike know that Jesus was persecuted for what he believed and for what he taught, for confronting evil face to face. We turn next to Jesus the suffering servant.

CHAPTER FIVE

Jesus the Suffering Servant

> That they [the Jews] said (in boast) "We killed Christ Jesus the son of
> Mary the Apostle of God"; but they killed him not nor crucified him but
> so it was made to appear to them and those who differ therein are full of
> doubts with no (certain) knowledge but only conjecture to follow for of
> a surety they killed him not (Quran 4:157).

On the basis of this single verse in the Quran, many Muslims deny that Jesus was
crucified for the sins of humankind. But it is not that simple. Commenting on the
verse, Quranic commentator and translator Abdullah Yusuf Ali says "The end of
the life of Jesus on earth is as much involved in mystery as his birth" (Quran 4:157
note 663). There is *mystery* surrounding Jesus' death. In the Mel Gibson film, *The
Passion of the Christ*, the scene where Jesus is arrested is wrought with confusion, as
are many scenes that follow, especially Jesus carrying the cross through the streets of
Jerusalem and the crucifixion itself. The film probably does not even come close to
portraying the degree of confusion there must have been at the time of the events
themselves.

To the Christian, the passion and death of Jesus on the cross is central; it is
how God chose to redeem humankind from sin. There are several references in the
New Testament that support this belief (Matthew 26:28, Mark 14:24, Colossians
1:19–20, Galatians 6:14, 1 Corinthians 1:17–18), but none so specifically as 1
Corinthians 15:3–4: "For I delivered to you as of first importance what I also
received, that Christ died for our sins according to the Scriptures, and that He was
buried, and that He was raised on the third day according to the Scriptures." What
the Quran specifically says about the crucifixion is very brief, only the one verse
cited above. But what does it really say? What does it require of the faithful Muslim
who is bound to accept the Quran as revealed truth? It says that the Jews thought
that they had killed Jesus, or at least wanted to kill him, but they really did not. Does
this contradict the Christian belief? Not necessarily, even though some Muslim
commentators think that it does. Quran 4:157 points to doubts and uncertainty

over this issue. People of both faiths recognize that there is mystery involved here. What really did happen on Good Friday and why? Who was responsible? Who was *ultimately* responsible? Perhaps meditative reading of both scriptures, guided by some exegetical commentary, can be mutually informative and, if not eliminate the mystery, at least enrich its meaning.

WHAT REALLY HAPPENED ON GOOD FRIDAY?—THE MUSLIM BELIEF(S)

Muslim commentators from very early on have explained the event of the crucifixion in a number of ways. But let's be clear on one thing. They all agree that a crucifixion took place, that *someone* was crucified. Many have said that someone other than Jesus died on the cross; a substitute was provided. Bear with me here as we look at several of these commentators, some in detail.[1] Each one that we have chosen to examine adds elements to the story that are interesting to Muslim and Christian alike, elements that help us contemplate the intriguing events that must have happened on that fateful Friday in Jerusalem. A Christian apologist[2] and a Muslim apologist[3] both agree that even the apostles must have been confused and bewildered by what was happening all around them and to them. It would take time and someone like the apostle Paul to explain it all to them later on, after the fact.

The earliest written commentary on Quran 4:157 is by Muhammad al-Kalbi (d. 763) who in turn relied heavily on Ibn 'Abbas (d. 687). That account goes like this:

> Because of their saying we killed the messiah Jesus son of Mary, the messenger of God, God destroyed one of their [the Jews'] friends, Natyanus, but they killed him [Jesus] not, nor did they crucify him, but so it was made to appear to them, the likeness [*shibh*] of Jesus was cast upon Natyanus, so they killed him instead of Jesus, and those who differ therein about his killing are full of doubts about his killing; they have no knowledge concerning his killing, only conjecture.[4]

This account clearly endorses the substitution theory.

A more popular version of the substitution narrative, in fact the most popular version, is based on the authority of Wahb Ibn Munnabih and is reported by the famous early Arab historian and commentator al-Tabari (d. 732):

1. Benjamin Todd. Lawson, "The Crucifixion in the Qur'an and Qur'anic Commentary: A Historical Survey," *Bulletin of the Henry Martyn Institute of Islamic Studies* 10, issue 2, 34–62 and issue 3, 6–40 (Hyderbad, India, 1991). This is an excellent, detailed discussion of Quranic commentary on the crucifixion.
2. Parrinder, *Jesus in the Qur'an.*
3. Hussein, *The City of Wrong*, 331.
4. Cited in Lawson, "The Crucifixion in the Qur'an," issue 2, 45–46.

It happened that Jesus was in a house with seven disciples when the Jews surrounded them. When the Jews entered the house, God changed all of the disciples to look like Jesus. The Jews, claiming they had been bewitched, demanded that Jesus be pointed out to them, otherwise they would kill all of them. Jesus then said to his disciples, "Who would purchase for himself paradise today?" One of them volunteered, announced to the Jews that he was Jesus, and was killed and crucified by them. Thus it appeared to them; and they thought that they had killed Jesus, and the Christians like-wise thought that he was Jesus, and God raised Jesus on that day.[5]

Al-Tabari reports a longer, much more detailed variant to Ibn Munnabih's substitution account:

When God revealed to him that he would soon leave the world, Jesus became troubled. He gathered his disciples for a meal. Jesus served them, washing their hands and drying them with his garment. The disciples recoiled at this, thinking it to be beneath Jesus. Jesus chided them for their reaction, telling them they should sacrifice them selves for each other as Jesus has sacrificed his self for them. Then he said: "Pray fervently to God that my death be postponed." They began to pray but were unable to fend off sleep, it being late. Jesus aroused them, scolding them for sleeping. Then he said: "When the shepherd disappears, the flock scatters. The truth is, one of you will deny me before the cock crows three times. And one of you will sell me for a paltry price..." The Jews then dispersed.

The Jews were looking for Jesus and encountered Simon Peter. They accused him of being a disciple, which he denied; they met another disciple and the same thing happened. The cock crew, reminding him of Jesus' warning, and he was saddened. Then one of the disciples came to the Jews and offered to lead them to Jesus for a price. At some point this disciple was changed into the likeness of Jesus, so the Jews took him, sure that he was Jesus. They bound him and led him around, saying: "You have raised the dead, driven away devils, and cured the insane; why not therefore free yourself from this rope?" The Jews spat upon him and placed thorns upon his head. When they came to the post upon which they intended to crucify him, God raised him, and they crucified what appeared to them. And he remained crucified seven hours.

Then Jesus' mother, and the woman he had treated and whom God had freed from madness, came weeping before the crucified one. Jesus appeared to them and asked them why they were weeping. They said, "For you." He said: "Verily, God has raised me to Himself, and nothing but good can befall me. This thing only appears so to them; so, send for the disciples that they may meet me at such-and-such place."

Eleven disciples met him at the designated place. Jesus discovered that

5. Ibid., 47.

the one who had betrayed him was missing; upon inquiry he was told that he had repented and hanged himself. Jesus said: "If he repents may God forgive him." Then Jesus inquired about a youth who was following them. His name was Yuhanna and Jesus appointed him a disciple and instructed them all to preach to the people in their language and summon them.[6]

The first version of the story points to a voluntary substitute, chosen from Jesus' disciples. The second one describes a punitive substitution, the traitor Judas who turned Jesus in to the Jewish authorities. Judas's appearance was then altered, according to the story, so that he looked like Jesus. Judas was apprehended by the authorities who then tied him up, tried him and crucified him instead of Jesus. What quickly becomes obvious in this second account is how closely several details echo what is reported in the gospels: the scene of the last supper; Jesus washing his disciples' feet (rather than hands); calling them to self-sacrifice as he sacrificed himself for them; asking the disciples to pray with him but their falling asleep instead; Jesus' prediction of Peter's denial before the cock crowed; Judas's betrayal for blood money; Jesus' mother and Mary Magdalene at the foot of the cross; and, finally, Jesus' appearance among the disciples following the crucifixion. Although Ibn Munnabih's reputation ranges from being "'trustworthy' to that of being an 'audacious liar,'"[7] his accounts exerted lasting influence on Muslim commentators and their forming an Islamic Christology. They were given enormous weight by the famous early Muslim exegete and historian al-Tabari whose commentaries we will examine in a moment.

Muhammad's biographer Ibn Ishaq (d. 767–68) offers his commentary on 4:157, although not in his famous biography of the prophet. He makes a big issue of the number of disciples who were with Jesus on the night before Good Friday. The Jews knew exactly how many there were, according to this version of the story, because they saw Jesus and his disciples earlier and counted them. But when they came to take custody of Jesus, there was one fewer—one of them was missing! Ibn Ishaq concludes that God must have already raised Jesus to Himself which would explain the missing person. Since the Jews did not know what Jesus really looked like and were afraid that they would not recognize him, they had offered Judas thirty pieces of silver to lead them to the disciples and point Jesus out to them. Judas was to identify Jesus by kissing him on the cheek, but he wrongly identified Serjes (Simon) as Jesus instead. The Jews didn't know any better. Judas then repented and hanged himself. The Christians cursed him, and some even believed that it was Judas who was crucified. Again, we see many details that confirm what we read in the gospels: thirty pieces of silver; identification and betrayal by a kiss; and Judas hanging himself.

6. Ibid., 47–48.
7. Ibid., 49.

Muqatil Ibn Sulayman al-Balkhi (d.767) identifies the substitute as a Roman soldier assigned to guard over Jesus. He was given the likeness of Jesus as punishment for assaulting the prophet and accusing him of blasphemy for claiming to be a messenger of God. Al-Balkhi then says, and this is really interesting, "those who differ therein (and) are full of doubts about the crucifixion are the Christians themselves." What he has in mind here is the confusion surrounding the events on Good Friday on the one hand, as well as confusion that arose amidst the emergence of various Christologies in the early centuries of Christianity on the other.

One Christian belief that could have contributed to, or at least echoes, the substitutionist theory is Docetism. Docetists believed that Jesus was totally divine, that he only *appeared* to have a human body. Thus, it only *appeared* that Jesus suffered, and it only *appeared* that he died on the cross. An early Christian text that supports this idea is the Apocalyptic Gospel of Peter, a text that was very popular and often referred to in early Christianity, and was even for a time considered by some churches to be a part of the New Testament scriptures.[8] Peter, who witnessed the crucifixion, said:

> What am I seeing, O Lord? Is it you yourself whom they take?...Who is this one above the cross, who is glad and laughing? And is it another person whose feet and hands they are hammering?
> The Savior said to me, "He whom you see above the cross, glad and laughing, is the living Jesus. But he into whose hands and feet they are driving the nails is his physical part, which is the substitute. They are putting to shame that which is in his likeness. But look at him and me.[9]

It is possible that Docetism had some influence on early Muslim commentators who developed a substitutionist theory to explain how it only appeared that Jesus died on the cross. On the one hand, it does provide an explanation for the phrase in the Quran "but so it was made to appear to them." But in another sense, Docetism is an unsatisfactory explanation for Islamic commentators. The Docetist argument depends on the total divinity of Christ and his illusionary humanity. Islam, on the other hand, believes solely in the humanity of Jesus and denies that he is God.

There are other early Muslim exegetes who present a substitution story, but a detailed description of each will not add any further to what we have already said about substitution as a theory to explain the crucifixion. So, we will move on to Muslim commentaries that offer still other possibilities. A brief but important commentary on the Quranic narrative of the crucifixion is attributed to the sixth Shi'ite imam, Ja'far Ibn Muhammad al-Sadiq. "Verily, we killed the Messiah," said al-Sadiq, although he did not tell us who "we" is. He does not explicitly deny

---

8. Ehrman, *Lost Scriptures*, 280.
9. Cited in Ehrman, *Lost Christianities*, 186–87.

the substitutionist theory, but he does say that "he [Jesus?] gained a high rank by being killed, just as God raised his other prophets. God seated him [Jesus?] on the throne of intimacy and reunion." What is most interesting about his commentary, though, is that it seems to affirm that Jesus was in fact killed and was thus spiritually exalted.

The first Muslim commentator to express doubt about the substitution theory is Abu Muhammad Abd Allah Ibn Muslim Ibn Qutaybah al-Dinawari (d. 889). Referring to the phrase, "But so it was made to appear to them," he said God meant that "They did not know about the killing of the Messiah with true knowledge, thoroughly comprehending the matter; rather it was conjecture." In other words, the Jews in Jerusalem were not fully aware of what their leadership had done—quite a departure from the interpretation reflected in the substitution theory. Another commentator to question the substitution theory is al-Tusi (d. 1068). He questioned whether or not it was even possible for one's likeness to be cast on another so that the two became indistinguishable. In the end, he decided that it is possible if God Himself chose to do so; thus, al-Tusi, in the end, accepts the substitution theory.

How much difference can the antecedent of a pronoun make? Abu 'l-Qasim al-Zamakhshari (d. 1144) challenged the substitution theory on grammatical and linguistic grounds. He was the first commentator to analyze the verses of the Quran using this technique, and he became one of the greatest exegetes of his time. He looked closely at the phrase "but so it was made to appear to them," and more specifically at a single word, the verb *shubbiha*. It is a form of the verb *shabbaha* and could be translated as "It was made similar to," or as the modern translator Abdallah Yusuf Ali translates it, "it was made to appear..." This word is crucial in the exegesis of this text; on it the substitution theory stands or falls. His question is what is the subject of the verb or, more specifically, the antecedent of the pronoun "it." There are three possibilities. Grammatically, it could be Jesus himself, but Jesus is the one who was resembled, not the one to be transformed in order to resemble Jesus. It could be the person who was killed, the substitute —if one accepted the substitution theory. But this person is nowhere mentioned in the text; the Quran nowhere identifies or even mentions the substitute. So, grammatically, he could not really be the antecedent of the pronoun; an antecedent should be somewhere in the text. A third possibility is that the verb is impersonal, that is, "it" (the event of the crucifixion) only seemed to them (to happen). In other words, they imagined it. Although al-Zamakhshari was apparently open to this last possibility, he ended up thinking that Jesus' appearance was projected onto someone else. The man who made al-Zamakhshari's commentary popular, al-Baidawi, said that such a substitution should be considered a miracle, possible only during the time of prophecy and only by the will of God.

Would God deceive mankind? Some one hundred and fifty years after al-Tusi questioned the substitutionist theory, the Asharite theologian Fakhr al-Din al-Razi picked up on his argument using the best of Greek logic. He claimed that transferring the identity of one man to another would open the door to sophistry; it would be deliberate deceit, and God is not open to that. The argument goes like this:

> so that if we saw Zayd, it would be possible that it was not really Zayd, but that the likeness of Zayd had been cast upon another. This would imply the nullification of social contracts such as marriage and ownership. Also it would lead to the impugning of the principle of *tawatur* [constancy], bringing into serious doubt all transmitted historical knowledge. This principle should be upheld as long as it is based on perceived phenomena. Such a confusion about perceived phenomena would threaten the foundations of all religious laws. Neither is it permissible to argue for such a transference of identity by appealing to the tradition which allows for miracles during the time of prophecy. Such a provision would bring into question the identity of the prophets themselves, which in turn would call into question the integrity of the sources of religious knowledge.[10]

Al-Razi responded to his own objection by saying that "God does have the power to give one person the appearance of another.... His intervention to save Jesus is, like all miracles, an exception. It should not therefore lead to generalized doubt."[11] In other words, according to al-Razi, God overrides the general rule and makes an exception in this particular case. But the point to make here is that al-Razi begins his inquiry from a position of doubt about the substitution theory.

Al-Razi raised several other objections to the substitution theory and then responded to each objection. For example, why, al-Razi asked, didn't God save Jesus more directly by having his angels just kill his enemies or by giving Jesus the power to repel them himself? Again, al-Razi answered this objection by pointing out that, "from an orthodox Muslim point of view, miracles require a specific divine intervention. They do not stem from a capability bestowed by God on a creature."[12] In other words, if God wanted to save Jesus, He (God) would have to do it directly. Jesus could not have saved himself. Another question raised by al-Razi: why did the disciples not remove all doubt by saying what really happened? This is exactly what Christians believe the disciples actually did. Al-Razi's answer: there were only very few people present at the event itself, and "if a universal tradition transmitted from generation to generation is based ultimately on the testimony of a very small

10. Cited in Lawson, "The Crucifixion in the Qur'an," issue 2, 13. Asharites were a school of early Muslim speculative theology founded in the tenth century.
11. Robinson, *Christ in Islam*, 137.
12. Ibid., 137.

group, it cannot be the basis of reliable knowledge."[13]

Al-Razi believed in letting the Quran comment on the Quran, that is, he sought to clarify verses in the Quran by referring to other verses. For example, he saw a possible source for the idea that Jesus sought a volunteer substitute in Quran 3:52 which says, "When Jesus found unbelief on their part he said: 'Who will be my helpers to (the work of) God?'" Could this be the basis for the Muslim tradition that Jesus asked for a volunteer to be taken by the authorities in his place? Another example, commenting on Quran 3:55, "Behold! God said: 'O Jesus! I will take thee and raise thee to myself and clear thee (of the falsehoods) of those who blaspheme,'" al-Razi cites Quran 35:10, "it is He Who exalts each Deed of Righteousness." Could this mean, al-Razi asks, that God raised Jesus' *deeds* to an exalted status?[14] What of the "falsehoods" mentioned in the verse? He cites two verses, Quran 26:27, "(Pharaoh) said: 'Truly your apostle who has been sent to you is a veritable madman!'" and Quran 15:10–11, "We did send apostles before thee amongst the religious sects of old. But never came an apostle to them but they mocked him." He cites these verses to support his opinion that the Jews, who did not accept Jesus as God's messenger, mocked Jesus by calling him "the apostle of God" (*rasul allah*) in the crucial verse 4:157. The context is important here. The verses that immediately precede and follow those that deal with the crucifixion condemn the Jews for various transgressions: idol worship (4:153), breaking their covenant, disbelieving revelation, slaying prophets (4:155), hindering others from God's way (4:160), taking usury (4:161). So, the theme of the verse about the crucifixion is not aimed at addressing the Christian view of the crucifixion per se, but rather should be seen as parenthetical and gratuitous, meant to underscore the vanity and futility of *kufr* (disbelief) among the particular Jews who mocked Jesus.[15]

Because of his method of raising objections and presenting a reply, it is not altogether clear what al-Razi's own personal opinion is about the substitution theory. What is clear is that he saw potential problems with the argument. But, in the end, the power of tradition in Islam is overwhelming. Al-Razi concludes that "as it has been solidly established by a decisive miracle that Muhammad is reliable in everything which he teaches us about Jesus, it is impossible that these questions, although they are entirely admissible, should become objections to the decisive text of the Quran." In other words, he accepts tradition on faith. Is this an endorsement of the substitutionist theory? Some say yes, but at least two modern scholars think that al-Razi's own view is too liberal to accept.[16] In fact, one of them goes so far as to say that "although he stops short of actually affirming the usual Christian idea

13. Ibid.
14. Lawson, "The Crucifixion in the Qur'an," issue 3, 31.
15. Lawson, "The Crucifixion in the Qur'an," issue 2, 37.
16. Robinson, *Christ in Islam*, 38 and Lawson, "The Crucifixion in the Qur'an," issue 3, 13.

that Jesus was put on a cross and killed, al-Razi...moves considerably towards such a position....What is curious, however, is that his commentary on this verse [4:157] has been virtually neglected by non-Muslims in their missionary efforts" and "has had so little influence on later Muslim exegetes."[17]

The Mu'tazilites, a "liberal" theology movement that emerged in the ninth century, questioned the substitution theory on moral grounds. As a movement, they have been considered by some modern Western scholars as free thinkers who, "if they had not been finally defeated and declared heretical by the eventually triumphant Sunni 'fundamentalists,' might have steered Islamic theology and thus life in a direction congenial, in fact amenable, to Christian convictions and interpretations."[18] When the Mu'tazilites considered the substitution of Jesus by another at the time of the crucifixion, it seemed to them that it would be unjust for God to allow someone to suffer in Jesus' stead. The very notion that God would commit acts of injustice, for any reason, was inconceivable to the Mu'tazilites. Furthermore, for God to allow such confusion of identity, for whatever reason, would be too irrational and therefore inadmissible. So, the Mu'tazilites categorically rejected the substitution theory.

Shi'ite authors would agree with the Mu'tazilites that God would not cause the substitution. Shi'ite authors, reporting on the authority of a Mu'tazilite theologian, Abu Ali al-Jubba'i (d. 915), report that Jesus was taken up to heaven by God. His absence now presented a problem. His enemies thought, according to this Shi'ite argument, that this rescue would stimulate even more support for his cause. So they, Jesus' enemies, captured a substitute instead, saying that it was Jesus, and crucified him. They let no one near the scene until the features of the person hanging on the cross had deteriorated beyond recognition. Those who later disagreed with this story, that is, those Christians who believed that Jesus did indeed die on the cross, were not among those who deceived the populace and crucified someone other than Jesus saying that it was Jesus. Although rejected by Christians and by many Muslims in the end, this is a very interesting argument; it makes all points of view *historically possible*. Those who killed "Jesus" (i.e., those who killed a substitute), those who believed that he was crucified and then resurrected and raised to heaven (i.e., most Christians), and those who believed that he was not crucified (i.e., many Muslims) could be correct. No mysterious or miraculous substitution would be required.[19]

During the tenth century, a small denomination of Muslims, the Brethren of Purity (*Ikhwan al-Safa*) came the closest to accepting the Christian narrative of the crucifixion. In their forty-fourth epistle, they say that Jesus' humanity was crucified

17. Lawson, "The Crucifixion in the Qur'an," issue 3, 13.
18. Mahmoud Ayoub, "Towards an Islamic Christology II," *Muslim World* 70 (1980): 101–2.
19. Robinson, *Christ in Islam*, 140f. and 171f.

and his hands were nailed to the cross. He was left there all day, given vinegar to drink, and pierced with a lance. He was taken down from the cross, wrapped in a shroud, and laid in a tomb. Three days later, he appeared to the disciples and was recognized by them. The night before the crucifixion, in the upper room, Jesus told his disciples that he was about to go away "to meet my Father and yours again." He said that he would depart "from my human form…. Those who accept my testament and are faithful to my pact will be with me tomorrow, but as for those who do not accept it, I shall not be of them at all, nor they of me…. For when I have departed from my human form I shall remain in the air at the right hand of the throne of my Father and yours and I shall be with you wherever you go."[20] It is clear in this epistle that Jesus' body was nailed to the cross, that he was placed in a tomb, presumably dead; and three days later, he was resurrected. He then seems to be announcing his ascension. If he is departing from his human form, to where/to what is he going?

"Behold!" God said, "O Jesus! I will take thee and raise thee to Myself." (Quran 3:55)

Some Muslims avoid the complications of the substitution theory by saying that Jesus was actually nailed to the cross, but that God rescued Jesus and raised him up literally from the cross. The rescue still poses important questions. Did Jesus die or was he taken up alive? Most Muslims believe that Jesus has died, or at least will die before the day of judgement. After all, Jesus himself said as an infant, "So peace is on me the day I was born, the day that I die, and the day that I shall be raised up to life (again)" (Quran 19:33). The question is when? There is also consensus among all Muslims that Jesus was taken up to heaven, but again, when, and in what sense, and under what circumstances? The ambiguity in the Quran, then, involves the distinction between resurrection on the one hand and ascension on the other. We will explore the answer to these questions in the chapter on resurrection, ascension and second coming.

What Do the Modern Commentators Say?

Several modern Muslim commentators stick to the substitution theory. Rashid Rida (d. 1935) studied with the well-known modern Egyptian reformer Muhammad Abduh. He read the verse (Quran 4:157) "but they killed him not nor crucified him" literally; the Jews did not kill Jesus. They thought that they had killed him, but what really happened, they are not sure. "And those who differ therein are full of doubts with no (certain) knowledge." After all, most Jews did not really know Jesus, let alone what he looked like. It would have been easy enough for them to take someone else thinking it was Jesus. Rida endorses the substitution theory; and

20. Ibid., 57.

then he moves on to what seems to be the main purpose of his commentary, to attack the idea of vicarious redemption in Christianity. He says that the four gospels have been poorly transmitted and that many important sources have been lost or destroyed. He is the first Muslim commentator to refer to the Gospel of Barnabas, a source which would become the primary text for Muslim commentators refuting Christianity. A most conspicuous theme in the Gospel of Barnabas is the frequent foretelling of Muhammad, often with explicit mention of his name. When that gospel was written is unclear. The first reference to it goes back to an Italian monk in the late sixteenth century who found the manuscript in the papal library of Sixtus V. It was not until the early twentieth century, though, that the manuscript was translated from Italian into English, and then into Arabic. The gospel tells the story of Jesus in twenty-two chapters. In the passion story, Jesus' likeness is cast upon Judas who is crucified in his place. Jesus is rescued by God, through a window in a house where he has taken refuge, and installed in the third heaven until the end of time.

Another modern Muslim commentator who adds something new to the picture is Abu al-Mawdudi (d. 1979). Like many other commentators, classical and modern, he writes that Jesus was rescued from crucifixion, and that both Christians and Jews are wrong in believing that he died on the cross. The interesting point that Mawdudi adds, however, is this: it is clear from "a comparative study of the Quran and the Bible...that most probably it was Jesus himself who stood his trial in the court of Pilate."[21] That Jesus had no substitute at least this far into the story is important. What the gospels say about the trial has a lot to do with the ultimate consequences of the passion story. We'll come back to this. Mawdudi does not rely on the Gospel of Barnabas but does say that the very existence of so many versions of the story proves that no one had definite knowledge of what really happened.

There are, on the other hand, several modern Muslim writers who have studied the Quran and do not believe that it denies the crucifixion. Their goal is to try to understand the basis for Muslim rejection of the crucifixion, reasons which are based on a particular reading of the text of the Quran and not supported conclusively by the text itself. A twentieth-century Egyptian author, Muhammad Kamel Hussein, writes that "the idea of a substitute for Christ is a very crude way of explaining the Quranic text. They [early Muslim scholars] had to explain a lot to the masses. No cultured Muslim believes in this nowadays."[22] Though, I'm not sure this last statement is correct. A few years ago, I gave a talk to a large group of Muslims—well over fifty of them—in Manassas, Virginia. After introducing the topic of the crucifixion and Quran verse 4:157, I asked if anyone believed that Jesus was crucified. No one raised a hand. I waited several seconds to see what

---

21. Quoted from Lawson, "The Crucifixion in the Qur'an," issue 3, 22.
22. Hussein, *The City of Wrong*, 331.

would happen. Finally, one man raised his hand and said that he believed that Jesus was crucified, but then God rescued him from the cross. Then a few others raised their hands and described some variant to Jesus being taken from the cross, either alive or dead. Most of the Muslims present believed in the substitution theory; but they represented a full range of variants to that story.

Who Killed Jesus?

One day while I was riding on the train with my good friend Abdallah, a very pious Muslim who knows the Quran very well, I asked him if he knew the verse in the Quran that spoke of Jesus' crucifixion. He did know it and recited it aloud without hesitation: "they killed him not nor crucified him but so it was made to appear to them and those who differ therein are full of doubts with no (certain) knowledge but only conjecture to follow for of a surety they killed him not (Quran 4:157). When I asked him to back up to the beginning of the verse, again he did without hesitation: "They [the Jews] said (in boast) "We killed Christ Jesus the son of Mary the Apostle of God." Then he stopped short and said, "Wow! This raises a whole new question." If the Jews did not kill Jesus, then who did? This is an entirely different question than whether or not Jesus was really killed. Quran 4:157 states that *the Jews* did not kill Jesus; it does not have to be read as a denial of the crucifixion.

Many Muslims acknowledge that it was Jesus himself, not a substitute, who stood trial in person before Pontius Pilate. Refer back to the commentator Mawdudi. Jesus himself, not a substitute, stood trial before Pilate. The scene is not described in Muslim scripture, but it is described in considerable detail in the Bible. In fact, Jesus stood before Pilate twice. The first time, as described in the Gospel of John, Pilate said to Jesus' accusers, "Take Him yourselves, and judge Him according to your law." The Jews said to him, "We are not permitted to put anyone to death" (John 18:31). So, who is the agent of crucifixion? Not Jesus' Hebrew contemporaries. They were among those who condemned Jesus, but they recognized that they did not have the authority to crucify him. So they took him to Pontius Pilate.

The Roman authorities then? Pilate made it very clear that "I am not a Jew" (John 18:35). After Jesus was flogged and the soldiers placed a crown of thorns on his head, Jesus was brought back before Pilate again. This time, Pilate said "Do you not know that I have authority to release you, and I have authority to crucify you?" Jesus answered, "You would have no authority over me, unless it had been given you from above" (John 19:10–11). Jesus told Pilate that this was all part of God's plan. Matthew's gospel tells us that it was foretold in the Old Testament, and therefore has to have happened that way (Matthew 26:54), in other words, it was determined by God. Peter reminds the disciples in Acts 3:18 (NIV) that "this is how God fulfilled what he had foretold through all the prophets, saying that his Christ would suffer." Acts 4:27–28 (NIV) makes it even more clear. "Indeed Herod and Pontius Pilate met together with the Gentiles and the people of Israel in this city to conspire against your holy servant Jesus, whom you anointed. They did what your power and will had decided before hand should happen."

The Quran also acknowledges God's power and authority over the life of Jesus:

> In blasphemy indeed are those that say that God is Christ the son of Mary. Say: "Who then hath the least power against God if his will were to destroy Christ the son of Mary his mother and all everyone that is on the earth? For to God belongeth the dominion of the heavens and the earth and all that is between. He createth what he pleaseth. For God hath power over all things" (Quran 5:17).

The first sentence in this verse challenges the Christian concept of the trinity, and we will have to return to that in the chapter on the trinity. What is relevant to our discussion now, though, is that God, and only God, has the authority to give and to take life, including the life of Jesus. So, when the Quran says "but they killed him not nor crucified him," could it mean that God and not man is the author of this quintessential sacrifice?[23]

THE CITY OF WRONG—
JERUSALEM, CIR. AD 33, THE FRIDAY BEFORE PASSOVER, GOOD FRIDAY

If the Jews did not kill Jesus, then who did? We all did, argues Muhammad Kamal Hussein, all of humanity who have ever committed sin. Dr. Hussein was a surgeon by profession. But, he became well known and widely read in Egypt and internationally for his writing on Islamic history, philosophy, and literature, but especially for his book *The City of Wrong* (*Qaryat dhalima* in Arabic). A devout Muslim, he had many Christian friends in Egypt as well as in the West. He was deeply committed to international peace movements and to Christian–Muslim dialogue. The City of Wrong is Jerusalem. The Arabic word that is translated here as "city" (*qaryat*) really means small town or rural community rather than city; Dr. Hussein chose this word because it could mean anywhere where people act against their conscience, that is, commit sin. *Dhalima* means iniquitous, dark in the most sinister sense of the word. The idea is scriptural: "How many populations have We destroyed which were given to wrong-doing? (*min qaryatin 'ahlaknaahaa*)" (Quran 22:45), "how many were the populations we utterly destroyed because of their iniquities (*min qaryatin kaanat*) setting up in their places other peoples?"

---

23. If one accepts this as true, then the Roman executioners and even Judas are mere accomplices. One of the arguments in the Gospel of Judas is that Jesus asked Judas to betray him. Rodolphe Kasser, Marvin Meyer, and Gregor Wurst, eds., *The Gospel of Judas* (Washington, DC: National Geographic, 2006).

(Quran 21:11). Jesus conveys this same idea in a parable in the Gospel of Matthew, chapter 21. A landowner rented his vineyard to vine growers and left on a journey. In his absence, vine growers mistreated and killed the landowner's slaves and even the landowner's own son. After the story, Jesus says "Therefore I say to you, the kingdom of God will be taken away from you (the wrongdoers), and be given to a nation producing the fruit of it" (Matthew 21:43). In the next chapter, Jesus says "But the king was enraged and sent his armies, and destroyed those murderers, and set their city on fire" (Matthew 22:7).

Dr. Hussein's story takes place on the Friday of the crucifixion, Good Friday. The author remains, in his own mind, faithful to the text of the Quran. Nowhere does he describe the actual crucifixion of Jesus, nor does he deny that it happened. In fact, Jesus remains in the shadows throughout the book, although we learn that he was accused of blasphemy and treachery, arrested, tried and condemned to death by the city's authorities with the collaboration of the Roman occupation government. The people we do meet, whose minds we enter, are the man who forged the nails that would be driven through the hands and feet of the victim, the man who was raised from the dead by Jesus and who enters the blacksmith shop, the head priest who is the spokesman for the prosecution, the Roman governor Pilate, and the soldiers who are assigned to guard the prisoner and to execute the sentence that is imposed.

> On that day the Jewish people conspired together to require from the Romans the crucifixion of Christ, so that they might destroy his message. Yet what was the mission of Christ save to have men and women be governed by their conscience in all they did and thought? When they resolved to crucify him it was a decision to crucify the human conscience and extinguish its light.... On that day certain men willed to murder their conscience and that decision constitutes the supreme tragedy of humanity. That day's deeds are a revelation of all that drives us into sin."[24]

The story does not cast judgment on any particular person, or even on any particular group, but rather on all of humanity. What happened in Jerusalem on that day was a repeatable and, in fact, often repeated act. It had happened many times before and would happen again in any "city" large or small, wherever humanity chooses to act against its conscience, whenever it chooses wrong over the message brought by Jesus. So, in a sense, Jesus died *because* of our sins but not to *pay for* our sins.

WHY THE AMBIGUITY?

There is obviously ambiguity in the Quranic text, evidenced in the range of views expressed by the commentators as well as among all Muslims. Many, if not

24. Hussein, *The City of Wrong*, 29–30.

most, Muslims still believe that Jesus was substituted on the cross, even though the Quran nowhere identifies who the substitute is or specifies that a substitution took place. The question that remains is: why do Muslims cling to the idea of substitution? Benjamin T. Lawson suggests it is because that is an easy way to deny the crucifixion, which in turn is a way to deny that Jesus vicariously redeemed mankind from sin (i.e., *paid* for our sins) by his death on the cross, the belief that is at the very center of Christianity. It is really a denial of vicarious atonement for our sins.[25] We turn next to the Christian and Muslim concept of sin.

25. Lawson, "The Crucifixion in the Qur'an," issue 3, 28–30.

CHAPTER SIX

Atonement—Salvation

SIN

Sin is the reason that the crucifixion is so important. There are different views of just what sin is. Does sin consist if doing an evil deed, or is it a state of being? The Bible actually supports both of these notions. Psalm 25:7 separates our sinful deeds from our person, or at least petitions God to separated them: "Remember not the sins of my youth and my rebellious ways; according to your love remember me." In the New Testament, 1 John 3:4 equates sins with breaking the law: "Everyone who practices sin also practices lawlessness; and sin is lawlessness." Sin results in a state of being that is akin to sickness or even death: "So also I will make *you* sick, striking you down, desolating *you* because of your sins" (Micah 6:13). Paul tells us in his letter to the Ephesians: "you were dead in your trespasses and sins" (Ephesians 2:1). A few verses further, Paul describes the state of being that results as being "separate from Christ, excluded from the commonwealth of Israel, and strangers to the covenants of promise, having no hope and without God in the world" (Ephesians 2:12). When sin is seen as acts or deeds, some Christians see a range in the gravity of sins; they distinguish between mortal sins and venial sins, the former being fatal to one's relationship with God. On the other hand, some Christians see *all* sin as equally fatal in that relationship.

The Muslim concept of sin is essentially the same. Quran 2:229 says that: "These are the limits ordained by God; so do not transgress them. If any do transgress the limits ordained by God such persons wrong (themselves as well as others)." Muslims, like Christians, are taught that sin produces an unfavorable state of being, one that we would be ashamed of, no less. A *hadith* of Sahih Muslim states that "sin is that which causes discomfort within your soul and which you dislike people to become informed of."

ORIGINAL SIN

Most Christians would say that they believe in original sin. Most Muslims would say that they do not. But what exactly is it that most Christians believe original sin is? And what exactly is it that most Muslims reject about original sin? When we start to articulate an answer to these questions, we discover that there is a wide range in beliefs in both religions. And once again, if we reduce the "Christian" belief and the "Muslim" belief to absolute "truth" statements, there is direct contradiction. But when we examine the wide range of interpretations within each faith, we find that they are less in direct opposition.

What is original sin? One of the simplest, most straightforward answers to that question is perhaps the one found in the Baltimore Catechism, the official catechism of the Roman Catholic Church in America:

> Q. What is the sin called which we inherit from our first parents?
> A. The sin which we inherit from our first parents is called Original Sin.
> Q. Why is it called Original Sin?
> A. this sin is called original because it comes down to us from our first parents, and we were brought into the world with its guilt on our souls.[1]

Original sin is, first, the sin that Adam and Eve committed; and, as far as the rest of humanity is concerned, a consequence of this first sin—the hereditary stain with which we are born on account of our origin or descent from Adam. Said another way, original sin is the privation of sanctifying grace in consequence of the sin of Adam and Eve. Original sin, then, stems from the sin of Adam and Eve that is described in Genesis, chapter 3, eating from the forbidden tree. As a consequence, Adam and Eve were expelled from the garden and were, so to speak, sentenced to a life of hard labor. Genesis does not specifically say that Adam and Eve's descendants inherit that sin. Although, the concept of original sin assumes that Adam and Eve's descendants are likewise banned from the garden.

The Apostle Paul adds another layer to the concept of original sin. "Therefore, just as through one man sin entered into the world, and death through sin, and so death spread to all men, because all sinned" (Romans 5:12). And a few verses further, "through the one man's disobedience the many were made sinners" (Romans 5:19). What exactly did Paul mean by this? Does it mean that every person born shares the guilt of sin even before

1. Thomas L. Kinkead, *An Explanation of the Baltimore Catechism of Christian Doctrine* (Rockford, IL: Tan Books and Publishers, 1988), 53.

that person commits any acts of sin of his/her own? Does it mean that Adam's sin brought sin into the world and so it is *inevitable* that human kind would sin? Does it mean that Adam's sin having caused sin to come into the world made sin a *possibility* for humankind? At best, exactly what Paul meant is ambiguous. There is nothing in the Romans passage to compel us to make the former interpretation—that sin is inevitable because of Adam. It is a possible interpretation, but not a necessary one.[2]

In the early fifth century, Saint Augustine removed the ambiguity for the Catholic Church. He said that human nature is tainted and corrupted by the sin of Adam, and this corruption is inherited from generation to generation much like genetic traits are passed down.[3] Original sin for Augustine, then, is not the same as actual sin, the sinful acts a person may do, but rather, an inclination to sin present in all people from birth.[4] It is in that sense that children are born in a state of sin. This became the official interpretation of the church at the Council of Carthage in 418, largely in criticism of Pelagianism, a Christian doctrine that believed that humans are created in the image of God and are good. Although they might be inclined to commit sins because they consistently follow Adam and Eve's precedent and bad example, humans still have the ability to choose between good and evil—a third possible interpretation of Paul.[5] As it turns out, humans, with the exception of Jesus and possibly Mary, have made some bad choices—have sinned. So, Pelagians would say, they need the atonement of Jesus Christ just as Adam did. Eastern Orthodoxy as well as many, if not most, Protestant churches take the position that humans merit death as a punishment of their own sins just as Adam merited it as the punishment for his sins, a position closer to Pelagianism than to Catholicism. Where there is agreement is in the need for atonement.

The Quran clearly rejects the idea of hereditary sin, the idea that people are born in a state of sin. "But if anyone earns a fault or a sin and throws it on to one that is innocent, he carries (on himself) (both) a falsehood and a flagrant sin" (Quran 4:112); and a few verses further, "Not your desires nor those of the People of the Book (can prevail): whoever works evil will be requited accordingly" (Quran 4:123). Abdallah Yusuf Ali's note for this verse says, "Personal responsibility is again and again insisted on as the key-note of Islam." Yet Muslims do agree that humans do have a tendency to sin, that in fact, all humans (with the exception of Jesus and Mary) do sin. "Nor do

---

2. *EFM (Education for Ministry) Year One: The Old Testament*, 3rd ed. (Sewanee, TN: The University of the South, 1999, reprinted in 2000 and 2002), 67–68.
3. Ibid.
4. *EFM (Education for Ministry) Year Three: Church History*, 4th ed. (Sewanee, TN: The University of the South, 2001, revised in 2003 and 2006), 195.
5. Ibid., 194.

I absolve my own self (of blame): the (human soul) is certainly prone to evil unless my Lord do bestow His Mercy: but surely certainly my Lord is Oft-Forgiving Most Merciful" (Quran 12:53). Still, Muslims believe that God's justice requires atonement for sin. One of several verses of the Quran that underscores this is: "So now has been proved true against us the Word of our Lord that we shall indeed (have to) taste (the punishment of our sins)" (Quran 37:31). Again, Abdallah Yusuf Ali's commentary: "God's decree of justice requires that every soul should taste the consequences of its own sins, and that decree must be fulfilled. No excuses can serve. It is only God's mercy that can save." God is the only recourse. The last part of verse 4:123 cited above reads: "Nor will he find *besides God* any protector or helper."

SIN OFFERING

The idea that sin, transgression, requires repayment was ingrained in the ancient Middle East. It was carved in stone in the Law Code of Hammurabi: "An eye for an eye, and a tooth for a tooth." In legal terms, it is described as the law of retribution. The offering of a sacrifice to redeem sin, a "sin offering," is not a new idea that came with Christianity. Offering sacrifices in ancient times was universal. All societies who somehow left traces of their history did it. There was no explanation needed; it was simply done. People offered sacrifices to commune with their gods, to offer praise and thanksgiving, to share a feast in the presence of the gods. Sometimes they offered sacrifices as gifts to the gods, sometimes to placate the anger of an offended deity, sometimes to ward off powers of evil or a pending disaster, often as a means of wiping away sin and removing pollution.[6] The ancient Hebrews offered sacrifices for all of those reasons. Until God allowed Abraham to offer a substitute sacrifice, Abraham's willingness to sacrifice his only son implies that sacrifice of the ancient Hebrews could even have included human sacrifice. Exodus 13:2 and 22:29 call for the firstborn to be offered to God. Leviticus 18:21 condemns the practice of child sacrifice. Leviticus 3 and 5 describe the communal sacrifices, called peace offerings in the Bible. These were feasts in which both God and the people partook. The idea that God ate his portion of the meal was prevalent in pagan cults, but is less emphasized in the Bible. But the Hebrews were told not to eat "any fat or any blood" (Leviticus 3:17) because "all fat is the Lord's" (Leviticus 3:16). They were not to eat blood because, as we will learn more in detail later, blood gives life. And Paul asks, "are not those who eat the sacrifices sharers in the altar?" (1 Corinthians 10:18). The Hebrews in Moses' time painted the blood of the sacrificed sheep

6. Frances M. Young, *Sacrifice and the Death of Christ* (London: SPCK, 1975), 21–30.

on the mantle of each doorway so that the shadow of death, sent by God, would pass them by (Exodus 12:1–36).

The law of retaliation was incorporated into the law of the ancient Hebrews. "But if there is any *further* injury, then you shall appoint as a penalty life for life, eye for eye, tooth for tooth, hand for hand, foot for foot, burn for burn, wound for wound, bruise for bruise" (Exodus 21:23–25, repeated in Leviticus 24:18–21 and Deuteronomy 19:21). When we read the law of retaliation in the Old Testament, it sounds like paying off the debt in kind, evil for evil. The New Testament clarifies the issue when Jesus said,

> "You have heard that it was said, 'An eye for an eye, and a tooth for a tooth.' But I say to you, do not resist him who is evil; but whoever slaps you on your right cheek, turn to him the other also. And if anyone wants to sue you, and take your shirt, let him have your coat also. And whoever shall force you to go one mile, go with him two. Give to him who asks of you, and do not turn away from him who wants to borrow from you. You have heard that it was said, 'You shall love your neighbor, and hate your enemy.' But I say to you, love your enemies, and pray for those who persecute you in order that you may be sons of your Father who is in heaven; for He causes His sun to rise on the evil and the good, and sends rain on the righteous and the unrighteous" (Matthew 5:38–45).

Evil is to be repaid with good, an idea that is not absent in the Old Testament. Leviticus 19:18 tells us, "You shall not take vengeance, nor bear any grudge against the sons of your people, but you shall love your neighbor as yourself." Jesus' role is to make this universal.

The Quran adds still another layer of importance to the concept. "We ordained therein for them: 'Life for life, eye for eye, nose for nose, ear for ear, tooth for tooth, and wounds equal for equal.' But if anyone remits the retaliation by way of charity, it is an act of atonement for himself. And if any fail to judge by (the light of) what God hath revealed they are (no better than) wrong-doers" (Quran 5:45). In the very next verse, God assigns a role for Jesus, "And in their footsteps We sent Jesus the son of Mary confirming the law that had come before him; We sent him the Gospel; therein was guidance and light and confirmation of the law that had come before him, a guidance and an admonition to those who fear God" (Quran 5:46). What is new here, what Jesus brought was "confirmation of the law." It's not just about you and me! It's also about the law, the well-being of the whole community, the state, the ruler, the holiness of God. That's why God cannot just forgive the debt outright. A few verses earlier, the Quran tells us: "On that account, We ordained for the children of Israel that if anyone slew a person unless it be for murder or for spreading mischief in the land, it would be as if he slew the whole people; and if anyone saved a life it would be as if he saved the life of the whole people. Then, although there came to them our apostles with clear signs yet even after that many of them continued to commit excesses in the land" (Quran 5:32).

So, in the end, what does God really want? Justice, integrity of the law and the community, the holiness of God on the one hand, and a restoration of the relationship between God and the sinner on the other. What God ultimately wants is a loving relationship with us. For that to be possible from the human side of it, He lovingly gave men and women the power to choose between right and wrong. And the unfortunate truth is that humans sometimes choose wrong—choose to pull back from that loving relationship with God. That is sin, the choice of wrong rather than right, and the consequent separation from God. That separation is deeply disturbing to God. The Bible is full of references to God's righteous anger: "for great is the wrath of the LORD that burns against us, because our fathers have not listened to the words of this book, to do according to all that is written concerning us" (2 Kings 22:13). There are fewer references to God's wrath in the Quran, but they're there: "So a wall will be put up between them (the good and the evil) with a gate therein. Within it will be Mercy throughout and without it all alongside will be (wrath and) Punishment!" (Quran 57:13). Abdallah Yusuf Ali's note to this verse points out that "Evil must realize that Good—i.e., Mercy and Felicity—had been within its reach, and that the Wrath which envelops it is due to its own rejection of Mercy." What God wants is for the relationship to be restored, bought back, redeemed. How can that be done?

After the Babylonian Captivity in the sixth century BC, when much of the kingdom and the temple itself had been destroyed and the people were carried off in captivity, the people thought that God's judgment on his disobedient people heightened the sense of national sin and emphasized the need for cleansing so that such a disaster would never happen again. Restoration would depend on removing the impurities. And the way to do that was through sin offerings, through sacrificial blood. Leviticus 17:11 is very clear: "For the life of the flesh is in the blood, and I have given it to you on the altar to make atonement for your souls; for it is the blood by reason of the life that makes atonement." Paul reminds us of this in his letter to the Hebrews: "And according to the Law, one may almost say, all things are cleansed with blood, and without shedding of blood there is no forgiveness" (9:22). From this time on, of all of the sacrifices offered in ancient times, sin offerings (Leviticus 4–7) became predominant among the Hebrews. These were the sacrifices that took center stage at the restored temple in Jerusalem during the time of King Herod, indeed when Jesus came to the temple.

But was blood sacrifice absolutely, *sine qua non*, necessary for forgiveness of sins? In the *Ryrie Study Bible*, the word "almost" in Hebrews 9:22 is in italics. The note to that verse says "For exceptions to the requirement of blood for cleansing permitted by the law, see Leviticus 5:11–13; Numbers 16:46; 31:50." Accordingly, exceptions to the requirement are allowed. The basic idea is for people to bring "as an offering to the Lord what each man found...to make atonement for ourselves before the Lord" (Numbers 31:50). Although God delights in sacrifices rightly offered, he makes it clear he prefers a contrite heart to the offering of sacrifice:

> For Thou dost not delight in sacrifice, otherwise I would give it;
> Thou art not pleased with burnt offering.
> The sacrifices of God are a broken spirit;
> A broken and a contrite heart, O God, Thou wilt not despise.
> By Thy favor do good to Zion;
> Build the walls of Jerusalem.
> Then Thou wilt delight in righteous sacrifices,
> In burnt offering and whole burnt offering;
> Then young bulls will be offered on Thine altar (Psalm 51:16–19).

The idea of a substitute to sin offerings was even more important after the destruction of the temple in the year 70; the sacrificial system that the Jews knew existed no more. At that time, Rabbi Joshua lamented "Woe to us, for the place wherein the sins of Israel were expiated is destroyed." But Rabbi Johanan Ben Zakkai was able to reply, "We still have a means of expiation of equal value, the practice of kindness, for it is said, 'I will have kindness, not offering'"[7]

WHO IS TO PAY OFF THE DEBT?

Obviously, the debtor is to pay off the debt; the sinner pays the debt of sin. This is why Muslims have a problem with the idea of vicarious atonement, with the idea of original sin, with the idea that someone other than the sinner pays off the debt. The Quran makes it quite clear that people are sinners and that they will bear the responsibility for their sins. Each sinner must pay for his or her own sins—at least to the extent that he or she is able to pay.

Fathi Uthman concedes that the concepts of salvation and redemption are difficult for Muslims, much more so than the crucifixion itself. On these issues, he recognizes that there are differences between Christianity and Islam, but he is quick to point out that both religions teach salvation through both

---

7. Quoted from Young, *Sacrifice*, 34.

faith and good works as he quotes Christian scripture: "What use is it, my brethren, if a man says he has faith, but he has no works? Can that faith save him?" asks the Epistle of James (2:14). For the answer, look in the Gospel of Matthew:

> "Not everyone who says to Me, 'Lord, Lord,' will enter the kingdom of heaven; but he who does the will of My Father who is in heaven. Many will say to Me on that day, 'Lord, Lord, did we not prophesy in Your name, and in Your name cast out demons, and in Your name perform many miracles?' And then I will declare to them, 'I never knew you; depart from Me, you who practice lawlessness'" (Matthew 7:21–23).

The Quran echoes the same idea, "Those who believe and work righteousness for them is forgiveness and a sustenance most generous" (Quran 22:50). The bottom line comes from the Lord's Prayer, "And forgive us our debts, as we also have forgiven our debtors" (Matthew 6:12). How often should we forgive someone who has sinned against us? "Seventy times seven times," Jesus says (Matthew 18:22). That forgiving others is a condition for being forgiven is made very clear in the parable of the lord who forgave the debt of his slave who could not pay, only to learn that the slave would not forgive the debt of his own debtor. The lord revoked his absolution. Jesus finished the story by saying: "My heavenly Father will also do the same to you, if each of you does not forgive his brother from your heart" (Matthew 18:23–35).

But the sad truth is that once the relationship with God is broken, it cannot be restored by man alone. Man simply does not have enough resources. In the Quran, God recognizes man's inadequacy. When God offered "the Trust" to all of creation, it was turned down. "But man undertook it (even though) he was indeed unjust and foolish" (Quran 33:72). And God does not demand from his creation more than it can do. Nowhere is that made more clear than in the Quran 2:286: "On no soul doth God place a burden greater than it can bear."

ONLY GOD CAN RESTORE THE RELATIONSHIP

God in his infinite mercy and love wants to be involved in restoring the relationship. Christians and Muslims believe that. The Muslim writer Mohamed al-Nowaihi writes, "...the way for the Muslim is there, in no one other than the Quran itself, which they believe to be the actual word of God....the Quran itself is nothing if it is not a suffering identity with creation and humanity. Hence its passion, its sorrow and chagrin for the disobedience and sins of man. *Ya hasratan 'ala l-ibad!* (Ah, alas [literally Oh, grief!] for my servants!) cries out a Quranic verse (Quran 36:30)."[8] The late Muslim

8. Mohamed al-Nowaihi, "The Religion of Islam. A Presentation to Christians," *International Review of Mission* 65 (1976): 221.

theologian Fazlur Rahman echoes al-Nowaihi. Describing man the sinner, Rahman says "God's role, His succor, His support ...are very crucial: no man can say 'I am going to be a good person' and automatically become one. He has to struggle, and in this struggle God is his willing partner."[9] God, through his divine word, comes to the rescue of sinning humans; God is the agent of salvation. "Those who listen to the *Word* and follow the best (meaning) in it, those are the ones whom God has guided" (39:18). The Quran teaches the faithful to pray: "Our Lord! condemn us not if we forget or fall into error; our Lord! Lay not on us a burden like that which Thou didst lay on those before us; our Lord! lay not on us a burden greater than we have strength to bear. Blot out our sins and grant us forgiveness. Have mercy on us. Thou art our Protector; help us against those who stand against faith" (Quran 2:286). The Quran offers assurance that God will answer that prayer. "If ye do love God, follow me; God will love you and forgive you your sins for God is Oft-Forgiving Most Merciful" (Quran 3:31). Every single *sura* of the Quran except for *sura* 9 begins with the words, "In the name of God the Most Gracious, the Most Merciful." We are saved by the mercy and grace of God. "Show us the straight way, the way of those on whom Thou hast bestowed Thy Grace" (Quran 1: 6–7).

Muslims believe that God saves us through his divine word. The guide for salvation, the "agent" of salvation if you will, is the Word of God as revealed through the Quran: "Those who eschew evil and fall not into its worship and turn to God (in repentance) for them is Good News: so announce the Good News to My Servants, those who listen to the Word and follow the best (meaning) in it; those are the ones whom God has guided and those are the ones endued with understanding" (Quran 39:17–18). Muslims believe that the Word (of God) became a book.

Christians believe that the Word became flesh, that God became man and came to earth to save us, that Jesus is the Word, and that "In the beginning was the Word, and the Word was with God and the Word was God" (John 1:1).

THE ACTIVE INGREDIENT IN BLOOD SACRIFICE?

This brings us back to the issue of sacrifice. What exactly is the active ingredient in the cleansing agent of the passion story? Is it the blood of the sacrificial victim? The Bible suggests that it is. "And according to the Law, one may almost say, all things are cleansed with blood, and without the shedding of blood there is no forgiveness." (Hebrews 9:22). In Old Testament times, it

9. Fazlur Rahman, *Major Themes of the Qur'an* (Minneapolis, MN: Bibliotheca Islamica, 1989), 21.

was the blood of animals. But from the time of Jesus on, the blood of bulls and goats was insufficient to take away sins. So, "if the blood of goats and bulls and the ashes of a heifer sprinkling those who have been defiled sanctify for the cleansing of the flesh, how much more will the blood of Christ, who through the eternal Spirit offered himself without blemish to God, cleanse your conscience from dead works to serve the living God?" (Hebrews 9:13–14).

How does this cleansing agent work? Is it the biological property of blood itself? "The life of the flesh is in the blood, and I have given it to you on the altar to make atonement for your souls; for it is the blood by reason of the life that makes atonement" (Leviticus 17:11). In other words, "as for the life of all flesh, its blood is *identified* with its life" (Leviticus 17:14).

How crucial is blood to blood sacrifice? In a classic work on the crucifixion, theologian P.T. Forsyth offers an answer. "It would have not have mattered a whit if no drop of blood had been spilt, if Jesus had come to his end by the hemlock or the gallows....Nor would it have mattered if, instead of losing but some of his blood, he had bled to death. Whether no blood was shed, or every drop, was immaterial." He explains that if the sacrifice depended on blood as blood, then the sacrifice might not have been complete if as much as a drop of blood remained in Jesus' body. On the other hand, if not a drop had been shed, there might not have been a sacrifice at all. "The value of the sacrificial rite," he writes, "lay wholly in the fact of its being God's will...what God ordained as the machinery of his grace....Everything for his purpose turns on the will to die."[10] In other words, it is not the blood per se, but rather God's will or willingness to shed it.

Jesus offered himself, his life without blemish, and without reservation. The active ingredient of the cleansing agent is Jesus' willingness to die for the sake of all of humanity, his consent to the sacrifice. Nowhere is that consent made more clear than in the Gospel of John: "For this reason the Father loves me, because I lay down my life that I may take it again. No one has taken it away from me, but I lay it down on my own initiative. I have authority to lay it down, and I have authority to take it up again. This commandment I received from my Father" (John 10:17–18).

Jesus' willingness to accept his own crucifixion, as willed by God, fulfills the whole of the Old Testament laws concerning sacrifice. It was a gift sacrifice of worship. It was a self offering as an act of obedience, like Abraham's willingness to sacrifice his son. His willingness was sufficient to demonstrate his obedience, and in itself was pleasing to God who then allowed Abraham a substitute sacrifice.

10. Peter T. Forsyth, *The Cruciality of the Cross* (London: Hodder and Stoughton, 1910), 177–79.

SACRIFICE IN THE QURAN

Sacrifice, in the sense that we are talking about in this chapter, appears in the Quran almost exclusively in the story of Abraham's sacrifice of his oldest son, mentioned several times, among them in *sura* 37:102–107:

> Then when (the son) reached (the age of) (serious) work with him he said: "O my son! I see in vision that I offer thee in sacrifice: now see what is thy view!" (The son) said: "O my father! do as thou art commanded: thou will find me if God so wills one practicing Patience and Constancy!"
> So when they had both submitted their wills (to God) and he had laid him prostrate on his forehead (for sacrifice)
> We called out to him "O Abraham!
> "Thou hast already fulfilled the vision!" thus indeed do We reward those who do right.
> For this was obviously a trial
> And we ransomed him with a momentous sacrifice.

The victim's name is different in the two traditions. In the Bible, the intended sacrifice is Isaac, son of Sarah. The Old Testament says his "oldest son Isaac." In the Quran, Abraham's son is not named, but he is identified in Islamic tradition as Abraham's oldest son Ishmael, son of Hagar. Muslim exegetes insist that Isaac was never the oldest son. How do we explain the discrepancy in the identity of the victim? Doesn't God know who the victim was? Could there be a human error in the recording of the name in the text? We know that humans played an active role in the actual, physical writing down of scripture. How important is the discrepancy? Very important— since Jews claim their descent through Isaac and Arabs through Ishmael. The importance of both lines of descent is clear in Genesis 21. In verse 12, God declares his promise to Abraham regarding Isaac, "God said to Abraham, 'Do not be distressed because of the lad and your maid; whatever Sarah tells you, listen to her, for through Isaac your descendants shall be named.'" We cannot stop reading there. The very next verse is God's promise to Abraham regarding Ishmael. "And of the son of the maid I will make a nation also, because he is your descendant [too]."

It could well be that placing all of the emphasis on the name of the victim misses the point of the whole story. What could be more important than the identity of the victim of Abraham's sacrifice? Abraham's obedience and willingness to sacrifice his son, of course. But also, the *victim's* consent to the sacrifice! The Muslim version of the story takes place in or near the city of Mecca where Hagar and Ishmael settled after Abraham sent them away. Abraham told Ishmael of God's command to the father to offer his son in sacrifice—and his son consented: "'O my son! I see in vision that I offer thee in sacrifice: now see what is thy view!' (The son) said: 'O my father! Do as thou art commanded: thou will find me if God so wills one practicing Patience and Constancy!'" (Quran 37:102). He offered to stand true to his promise if his self-sacrifice was really required. It is not sacrifice for sacrifice's sake. It is a test, an indication that the faithful will do what God really wants. Consent of the victim is the dimension that the Quran adds. Its actual recording in the Quran is subsequent to the time of Jesus, but the event that is described obviously happened long before Jesus' sacrifice. Could it be considered prophetic of Jesus' willingness to be sacrificed according to the plan that came down from above? In this case, God does not really want the flesh and blood of animals, much less of human beings. "It is not their meat nor their blood that reaches God; it is your piety that reaches him; He has thus made them subject to you that ye may glorify God for his guidance to you; and proclaim the Good News to all who do right" (Quran 22:37). What God really wants is the giving of our whole being to him, the symbol of which is that we should give up something very dear to us—an echo of what we read above in Psalm 51.

Quran 37:107 is an important verse: "And we ransomed him with a momentous sacrifice." Commenting on the adjective "momentous" that qualifies "sacrifice," Abdallah Yusuf Ali says that it is indeed a momentous occasion when two men with concerted will "ranged themselves in the ranks" of those who self-sacrifice themselves to God according to his divine will. It is in this sense that Jesus said, "He who has found his life will lose it, and he who has lost his life for my sake will find it" (Matthew 10:39). The first meaning of the Arabic word *fadanahu*, translated in verse Quran 37:107 as "ransomed" is actually "redeemed." God redeemed Abraham with this momentous sacrifice.

Redemptive Qualities of the Suffering Servant

To Jesus' disciples, and to all Christians from then on, Jesus' death gives a whole new meaning to sacrifice. Paul tells us in his letter to the Hebrews that "By this will [God's will] we have been sanctified through the offering of the body of Jesus Christ once for all" (Hebrews 10:10). And Jesus saw it coming. Jesus did announce his pending death to his disciples, that it was in fulfillment of a divine plan, and that it would ultimately triumph over evil in the world. While he was on his way to Jerusalem, walking with his disciples, he said, "Behold, we are going up to Jerusalem, and the Son of man will be delivered to the chief priests and the scribes; and they will condemn him to death, and will deliver him to the Gentiles. And they will mock him and spit upon him, and scourge him, and kill him, and three days later he will rise again" (Mark 10:33–34). During his last supper with his disciples, he linked his death with the figure of the perfect servant described in Isaac 53. "For I tell you, that this which is written must be fulfilled in me, 'And he was numbered with transgressors;' for that which refers to me has its fulfillment" (Luke 22:37).[11] Toward the end of the supper, Jesus said, "This is my blood of the covenant, which is poured out for many for forgiveness of sins" (Matthew 26:28). And he saw this as a "ransom for many" (Matthew 20:28 and Mark 10:45).

Jesus' consent to his own self-sacrifice is paramount. He says over and over again in the New Testament that he came to do the will of God. To cite just a couple of examples: "For I have come down from heaven, not to do my own will, but the will of him who sent me" (John 6:38) and "then he said, 'Behold, I have come to do thy will.' He takes away the first in order to establish the second" (Hebrews 10:9). He was obedient unto death. His consent to the crucifixion is dramatic. After Jesus and his disciples had their last Passover supper together, Jesus went to the garden of olives at Gethsemane on the west side of Jerusalem, high on a hill overlooking the city. He said to the three disciples who accompanied him, "My soul is deeply grieved, to the point of death; remain here and keep watch with me" (Matthew 26:38, Mark 14:34). Adding to his sorrow is that he felt so dreadfully alone, as he pleaded, unsuccessfully, that his disciples stay awake with him. He could not conceal his hurt. "Could you men not keep watch with me for one hour?" (Matthew 26:40, NIV). He was so deeply grieved that "being in agony, he was praying very fervently; and his sweat became like drops of blood, falling down upon the ground" (Luke 22:44). If Jesus did indeed sweat blood, a medical condition called hematidrosis, then his stress and trauma would have been extraordinarily intense.[12] Why such traumatic stress? Was he contemplating the intense suffering to which he was about to be condemned? As horrific as that suffering would have been—the unjust accusations before a series of religious and civil trials, five in all, three before religious courts and two before civil courts; the brutal scourging ordered by Pilate, what the Romans called "half-death;" the crowning of thorns; the humiliating march through the streets of Jerusalem; and, finally, the agony of the crucifixion itself—all of this in face of the sins of the world that this sacrifice would ultimately redeem

11. James Denney, *The Death of Christ: Its Place and Interpretation in the Bible* (London: Hodder and Staughton, 1909), 34 and note 1. Denney is among several scholars who make this connection. But Denney cautions that there are other scholars who question this.

12. William D. Edwards, Wesley J. Gabel, Floyd E. Hosmer, "On the Physical Death of Jesus," *Journal of the American Medical Association* 225, no. 11 (1986): 1456, cited in T. W. Hunt, *The Mind of Christ* (Nashville, TN: Broadman & Holman Publishers, 1995), 101–2.

was, at least for a moment, more than he could bear. So agonizing were those thoughts that Jesus cried out, "My Father, if it is possible, let this cup pass from me." (Matthew 26:39). The cup is the cup of his blood as he described during his last supper (Mark 14:23). This moment of reluctance was ever so brief, a sign of Jesus' humanness. In the very next breath, he affirmed his consent. "Yet not as I will, but as you will" (Matthew 26:39).

Jesus' consent is implied in the Quran.

> He said: 'I am indeed a servant of God. He hath given me revelation and made me a prophet; and He hath made me Blessed wheresoever I be and hath enjoined on me Prayer and Charity as long as I live; (He) hath made me kind to my mother and not overbearing or miserable; so peace is on me the day I was born, the day that I die, and the day that I shall be raised up to life (again)' (Quran 19:30–33).

Could the use of the term servant here be another link between Jesus the servant and the suffering servant in Isaiah 53? Theologian Julius Basetti-Sani thinks that it is precisely such a link.[13]

Jesus' suffering, his ultimate sacrifice, is becoming important to an increasing number of Muslim writers. In 1978, a professor of Arabic Language and Literature, Mohamed al-Nowaihi (d. 1981), wrote a paper (unpublished, but often quoted by scholars) entitled "Redemption: from Christianity to Islam." He describes redemption as:

> A symbol, but it stems from a record of facts—facts of certain individuals, in the long and tormented history of man, who were characterized by a tremendous love for their fellowmen and a chagrined concern over their ignorance, folly and crime, so much that they willingly suffered great persecution and were even ready to pay the supreme penalty of martyrdom for the sake of humanity's salvation.[14]

Let's consider some of those individuals in modern times who willingly suffered great persecution, even martyrdom for the sake of humanity's salvation, people like Mahatma Gandhi or Martin Luther King. How effective was their suffering in disarming the powers of oppression? How much more effective was the suffering of Jesus in the disarming of the evils of sin "When he had disarmed the rulers and authorities, he made a public display of them, having triumphed over them through him"(Colossians. 2:15)? In an earlier

13. Julius Basetti-Sani, "For a Dialogue," 191.

14. Quoted from Oddbjorn Leirvik, *Images of Jesus Christ in Islam* (Uppsala: Swedish Institute of Missionary Research, 1999), 183. A new edition of this work has just been released by Continuum International Publishing Group.

work, al-Nowaihi says "among the intelligentsia of contemporary Muslims there has been a growing awareness of the sheer beauty and nobility of the idea of redemption not, indeed, as a literal fact or an article of creed, but as a symbol." He continues, "This new development is prominent in the poetry of a new school of Arabic poets, which started in the late 1940's, and whose frequent use of the symbol of the cross and the figure of the Redeemer has caused much consternation among their traditionalist readers."[15] The symbol of the cross continues to resonate for at least this small number of Muslim poets.

15. Ibid.

Resurrection, Ascension, and the Second Coming

Peace is on me the day I was born,
the day that I die,
and the day that I shall be raised up to life (again) (Quran 19:33)

Courtesy of Jekyll Island Museum Archives.

Moments after his birth, according to the Quran, the baby Jesus spoke those words to those who had come to see him. Coincidentally, in Faith Chapel on Jekyll Island, Georgia, there is a remarkable stained glass window of the Birth of Jesus that could be said to reflect those same words. We see the Virgin Mary looking down at the baby Jesus in a loving, maternal gaze. Jesus is not looking at her; rather he looks at the three men who came to honor him. One is a richly dressed man who has laid before Jesus an incense burner made of gold. The second man is dressed like a Roman soldier. He is carrying a gold box, possibly containing myrrh. The third man, prostrating, face invisible, has in his left hand a crown of thorns. Far in the background, barely noticeable in the landscape, is a cave, possibly an open tomb? Joseph, not mentioned anywhere in the Quran, is absent from this glass window. It is almost as if Jesus is about to address the three men bearing gifts. In Islamic tradition, the Quran tells us that Jesus did speak as a newborn infant, almost immediately after his birth, as soon as Mary took him out and presented him to the people. He said: "Peace is on me the day I was born, the day that I die, and the day the I shall be raised up to life (again)." The four events—life, death, resurrection, ascension—although there is disagreement among the two faiths as to the exact sequence and timing, are inexorably linked. In both Christianity and in Islam, they climax in the second coming of Jesus at the time of judgment.

That the cross is essential to Christianity is quite clear, as we discussed in Chapter Five. As we have seen, one possible reason that many, if not most, Muslims do not accept the crucifixion is that they cannot accept the idea of vicarious atonement—that Jesus died in order to pay for our sins. But there is another reason. What many Muslims object to regarding that notion is that God would never have allowed a great prophet such as Jesus to die such an ignominious death. The Gospel of Matthew tells us that the Apostle Peter had exactly the same problem.

> From that time Jesus began to show His disciples that He must go to Jerusalem, and suffer many things from the elders and chief priests and scribes, and be killed, and be raised up on the third day. Peter took Him aside and began to rebuke Him, saying, "God forbid *it*, Lord! This shall never happen to You." (Matthew 16:21–22).

The very idea of Jesus being crucified was so revolting that Peter simply could not accept it. Peter believed that Jesus was the Messiah. Crucifixion would have been the end of it. God should not allow the Messiah to be crucified. Peter was pleading that the crucifixion not be allowed to happen.

Not too long ago, I had a conversation with my postman. He asked me if Muslims believe that Jesus died on the cross to save us. I answered that as a simple faith statement, Most Muslims did not. His comeback was that that the crucifixion is all that mattered and that was a major difference between Christianity and Islam. A major difference, yes, I agreed. But the only thing that mattered, not quite. As important to Christians as the crucifixion is, it is not the only the thing. If it were, if the crucifixion were not followed by the resurrection and the ascension, Christianity would have ended there.

Christians unanimously agree that Jesus died on the cross. But Christians believe that it did not all end there. *Resurexit sicut dixit* claims the Marian antiphon *Regina Caeli*; he arose *as he said he would*. I attended a Catholic high school, and I remember one of the priests who taught at the school built his Easter sermon around that Latin phrase. He put the emphasis on the last two words, *sicut dixit*, "as he said he would." The gist of the sermon was that the resurrection lent credibility to everything else in Christianity. Christianity would rise or fall on whether or not Christ rose from the dead.

DOES THE RESURRECTION NEED PROVING?

Because the resurrection, like the virgin birth, defies the way things normally happen, skeptics question whether the resurrection really happened or not. And because of the magnitude of its importance to Christianity, Christian apologists put forth a series of proofs to counter the critics.

One criticism is that we have no evidence of the resurrection other than what is written in the New Testament—the four gospels and the Acts of the Apostles and the writings of Paul, which, from the critics' point of view, are decidedly biased texts. What's more, there are several discrepancies in what these texts say. We have already discussed how the New Testament meets the criteria of historical soundness as well as, if not even better than, many historical texts of that era. Dr. Gregory Boyd, in his wonderful little book *Letters from a Skeptic* makes a convincing case that the New Testament's treatment of the resurrection passes the test even better than other parts of the New Testament itself. Descriptions of the resurrection are stylistically devoid of legendary material. New Testament descriptions report an amazing amount of detail, much of it incidental or even irrelevant to the story itself, which is characteristic of simply reporting eye-witness accounts. They include information that would actually be counter productive to a fabricated story, for example, reporting the prominent role of women in first discovering the empty tomb and being the ones to inform the other apostles. For the most part, first-century women played a secondary role at best in the public sector. They would have lacked credibility.

The "empty tomb" is often held up as evidence of the resurrection. But was it really empty? Again, the New Testament narratives all agree on that as fact. They point out that, fearing that the disciples might come to steal the body in order to claim that Jesus would rise from the dead as he said he would, the tomb was heavily guarded by Roman soldiers, making it impossible for the disciples to have taken the body. The disciples are the only ones who would have had any reason to steal it. Neither the Roman government nor the Jewish hierarchy could have possibly benefited from removing the body from the tomb. In fact, Matthew's gospel suggests that the chief priests were really surprised when the soldiers reported that the tomb was empty. The priests decided to explain away the empty tomb by conspiring to falsely accuse the disciples of stealing the body (Matthew 28:11–15). If the empty tomb were nothing more than a false claim—had the tomb not been empty—the body would have still been in it, a fact that could easily have been verified by going to look. Nowhere is it reported that anyone checked and found the body still there. The best evidence, on purely historical grounds, is that the tomb was really empty.

Perhaps even more difficult to explain than the empty tomb are the many post-resurrection appearances of Jesus. At least twelve, possibly more, such appearances are listed in the four gospels, Acts, and First Corinthians. First, Jesus appeared to Mary Magdalene, then to other women at the tomb on Easter morning, and then in the nearby garden (Matthew 28:1–10, Mark 16:1–8, Luke 24:1–12, and John 20:1–18). Then he appeared to two of his disciples on the road to Emmaus (Mark 16:12–13, Luke 24:13–32). In this case, the disciples did not recognize Jesus at first. Only after he sat and broke bread with them did they recognize him as the same man who, a few days earlier had taken bread, broke it, gave it to his disciples and said, "take, eat, this is my body." Luke 24:34 says that Jesus appeared to Simon Peter. Then Jesus appeared to the apostles in the upper room; Thomas was not there (Luke 24:36–43, John 20:19–25). When the apostles told him what they had seen, Thomas said he would not believe unless he touched the wounds of the resurrected Jesus, for which he became labeled by later Christianity "doubting Thomas." Maybe he just felt that he really missed something and now sought the full experience of it. A week later, Jesus appeared again to the apostles (Mark 16:14, John 20:26–31). This time, Thomas was there. Jesus invited Thomas to put his fingers into the nail holes in his hands and feet and his hand into his side that had been pierced by the lance. The gospel doesn't really say that Thomas actually did touch Jesus. Maybe he didn't. Maybe he just believed. For sure, he finally relished in the full experience of Jesus' resurrection as the other apostles had a week earlier. According to John, he did believe: "My Lord," he said, "and my God" (John 20:28).

While they were fishing, seven disciples saw Jesus at the Sea of Galilee (John 21:1–3). The eleven disciples saw Jesus on a mountain in Galilee (Matthew 28:16–20, Mark 16:15–18). Paul tells us that Jesus appeared to a crowd of five hundred people, "most of whom are still alive" (1 Corinthians 15:6, NIV). Paul wrote this letter around the year 55, approximately twenty years after the resurrection. His claim that most were still alive was probably true. It would have been hard to fabricate such a claim. Skeptics could have cross-examined at least some of them. But we have no record that any of them did.

"Then he appeared to James, and then to all the apostles, and last of all to me" (1 Corinthians 15:7–8, NIV). Here, Paul claims to have seen Jesus too. Is this a reference to his conversion experience which is reported in great detail in Acts 9:1–19, 22:3–16, 26:9–18)? If so, it is also a post-ascension vision. In any case, Jesus was seen one final time on the Mount of Olives, just before he ascended to heaven (Luke 24:44–49, Acts 1:3–8).

There are discrepancies in detail in these various accounts. Some people who are named in one account may not be named in another account of the same appearance. But any historical event reported by more than one eyewitness will have these kinds of discrepancies. Different people observe or remember different details. Some details will seem more important to some reporters than to others. When the different accounts agree on the central issues but differ on minor details, more than diminishing their credibility, they corroborate each other as independent sources.

There are two non-Christian texts that add to the corroborative evidence. Toward the end of the first century, the Jewish historian Josephus wrote:

> When Pilate, upon hearing him accused by men of highest standing among us, had condemned him to be crucified, those who had in the first place come to love him did not give up their affection for him. On the third day he appeared to them restored to life, for the prophets of God had prophesied these and countless other marvelous things about him.[1]

Dr. Edwin M. Yamauchi assesses this passage as "mostly authentic," except, perhaps, the reference specifically to the resurrection.[2] But he then goes on to another non-Christian text, that of the second-century Roman historian, Tacitus:

> Christus, from whom the name had its origin, suffered the extreme penalty during the reign of Tiberius at the hands of one of our procurators, Pontius Pilatus, and a most mischievous superstition, thus checked for the moment, again broke out not only in Judea, the first source of the evil, but even in Rome.

Yamauchi explains that this passage corroborates the crucifixion, but does not specifically mention the resurrection. Yamauchi suggests that the only way to explain the rise of such a mass movement as Christianity based on a crucified man is that it didn't end there; he rose from the dead.[3]

Jesus' apostles themselves were, at first, among the skeptics. After the crucifixion, they feared for their own lives and went into hiding. When the women came to tell them of the empty tomb, they had to come to see for themselves. But in the coming days, when they saw the empty tomb, when they saw Jesus in the flesh and shared food with him, saw him eat as only a

---

1. Cited in Strobel, *The Case for Christ*, 79.
2. Ibid., 80.
3. Ibid.

live person could, only then did they believe. And they did more than believe. They were transformed. They courageously accepted the great commission and went forth to teach what Jesus had taught them. And they did this at great cost to their own safety and well-being. No one experienced this radical transformation more than Paul himself. Before his conversion, Paul worked for the Jewish authorities enforcing the law. He was on a mission to route out the "heretical" sect who claimed to follow Jesus. Had Paul simply been interested in his own well-being, he would have continued to work for the Jewish establishment. Rather, he traveled all over the western Hellenistic world, tens of thousands of miles, to spread Jesus' teachings as he understood them. For that, he was beaten, imprisoned, and finally killed. He had been transformed.

The best explanation for all of this, based on a preponderance of historical evidence, is that it all really happened: the resurrection, the empty tomb, the post-resurrection appearances of Jesus, and the transformation of the disciples. N.T. Wright offers an interesting discussion of the convergence of faith and historical evidence. In the end, what people are willing to accept on the basis of historical evidence, or any evidence for that matter, is shaped by the worldview in which they live.[4] History can rarely *prove* anything. And it does not in this case. But it not only offers, at least to Christian apologists, the most likely explanation for the events; it challenges the skeptics to present more sound alternatives based on a preponderance of historical evidence, a task that is very difficult to do.

The debate about the resurrection is not especially important to Muslims. For those Muslims who do not believe that Jesus was crucified, the resurrection is a moot point. Those who do believe that Jesus was nailed to the cross move from there right on to God raising Jesus up to Himself as it says in Quran 3:55: "I will take thee and raise thee to Myself." The question is: was Jesus rescued or raised before dying, instead of dying, or after dying? If it was the last, then Jesus would have been raised from the dead—resurrection. In either of the two other scenarios, Jesus at least ascended to heaven. And it is the ascension of Jesus which most interests Muslims. In addition to Quran 3:55 cited above, Jesus says in Quran 5:117: "when Thou didst take me up, thou wast the Watcher over them and Thou art a Witness to all things." In both these verses, the meaning remains ambiguous. In fact, Tarif Khalidi's translation reads, "when you *caused me to die* [emphasis added]," instead of "when Thou didst take me up." We may not be able to find a definitive answer to these questions, but we can examine what classical Muslim commentators

4. N.T. Wright, *Surprised by Hope: Rethinking Heaven, the Resurrection, and the Mission of the Church* (New York: HarperCollins, 2008), 58–65.

on the Quran had to say about it. No fewer than five classical commentators give no fewer than ten different interpretations to those two verses.[5]

Al-Tabari reports on the authority of al-Rabi Ibn Anas (d. 756) that God meant "I am going to cause you to sleep and raise you to myself while you are asleep." This interpretation is linked to two other verses in the Quran:

> It is He Who doth take your souls by night and hath knowledge of all that ye have done by day. By day doth He raise you up again; that a term appointed be fulfilled; in the end unto Him will be your return then will He show you the truth of all that ye did."(Quran 6:60).

and

> It is God that takes the souls (of men) at death: and those that die not (He takes) during their sleep: those on whom He has passed the decree of death, He keeps back (from returning to life) but the rest He sends (to their bodies) for a term appointed. Verily in this are Signs for those who reflect." (Quran 39:42).

Along with this commentary, al-Rabi reports the following tradition (*hadith*) of the Prophet Muhammad, "The Messenger of God (the peace and blessings of god be upon him!) said to the Jews, 'Jesus did not die (on the cross). He will return to you before the day of the resurrection.'" The implication is that Jesus only seemed to have died; he was really only asleep.

According to another commentary reported by al-Tabari, attributed to several different authorities, God meant, "I am going to grasp you from the earth and raise you to Myself." Like the first interpretation, the implication here is that Jesus had not died, but rather was taken up to God *alive*.

A third interpretation reported by al-Tabari, based on three traditional authorities, says that God clearly meant that Jesus died. "I am going to cause you to die," God said, "and raise you to myself." But when? Al-Tabari reports still a fourth interpretation according to which God meant, "I am going to raise you to myself and purify you from those who disbelieve and cause you to die *after* sending you back down to the world," in other words, after the second coming. But that interpretation is refuted by the late rector of Al-Azhar University, Dr. Mahmud Shaltut, who said:

> the expression *tawaffaitani* is entitled in this verse to bear the meaning of ordinary death....There is no way to interpret "death" as occurring after his return from heaven in the supposition that he is now alive in heaven, because the verse very clearly limits the

---

5. For a more detailed description of these commentaries, see Robinson, *Christ in Islam*, 117–26. The summary that follows is based on Robinson.

connection of Jesus to his connection with his own people of his own day, and the connection is not with the people living at the time when he returns.... All that the verses referring to this subject mean is that God promised Jesus that he would complete for him his life-span and would raise him up to himself.[6]

Three commentators other than al-Tabari favor yet another interpretation. God meant, "I am holding you back from being killed by the unbelievers and causing you to tarry until the term I have decreed for you and causing you to die by natural causes not by being killed at their hands." This interpretation deals with the concern that it would not have been fitting for Jesus to have been crucified as it is described in the gospels, that God rescued Jesus, and that Jesus would die a natural death at some later time.

Sufis, Muslim mystics, tend to prefer yet another interpretation, the interpretation where God said, "I am going to receive (or take) you away from your desires and the pleasures of your carnal soul." Jesus' humanness, his human desires such as anger, lust, all other human traits, would be extinguished. God would destroy in Jesus all the desires which prevent ascent to the world of the spirits. What would remain? His soul? His divine attributes? This interpretation separates the body from the soul; it separates the human from the non-human.

In contrast, one commentator, al-Razi, reports that God specifically took Jesus, all of Jesus. That's why he chose the word *tawaffa* which means "to claim in full. "He links this to another verse in the Quran (4:113) "to thee they can do no harm in the least." Al-Razi reports yet another interpretation whereby what God raised unto Himself was not Jesus' being, but rather his work, his deeds, his merit, or his honor. Again, he links this to another Quranic verse (35:10): "Who so desireth power (should know that) all power belongeth to God. Unto Him good words ascend, and the pious deed doth He exalt."[7]

The ambiguity in the Quran, then, involves the distinction between resurrection on the one hand and ascension on the other. If Jesus was taken up to heaven after he died, that is ascension *after* resurrection. If he was taken up before or instead of death, that is simply ascension. In the final analysis, whether or not Muslims believe that Jesus had already died and resurrected from the dead, at the very least they believe that God raised him to heaven, that is, they accept his ascension.

Compared to the resurrection, the ascension of Jesus in Christian tradition seems to be understated, the two events sometimes even collapsed into one.

---

6. Quoted from Parrinder, *Jesus in the Qur'an*, 115–16.
7. I use the Pickthal translation here because, in my judgment, it gives more meaning to this interpretation of Quran 3:55 and 5:117.

N.T. Wright stresses that scripture does not allow this. The ascension has its own distinctive meaning and importance.[8] It addresses the issue of what happened to Jesus after his historical presence here on earth. Where did he go? Where is he now? What role does he play for Christians today, or for Muslims too for that matter?

The principle New Testament text that describes the ascension is Acts 1:3–10, NIV:

> After his suffering, he showed himself to these men and gave many convincing proofs that he was alive. He appeared to them over a period of forty days and spoke about the kingdom of God. On one occasion, while he was eating with them, he gave them this command: "Do not leave Jerusalem, but wait for the gift my Father promised, which you have heard me speak about. For John baptized with water, but in a few days you will be baptized with the Holy Spirit." So when they met together, they asked him, "Lord, are you at this time going to restore the kingdom to Israel?" He said to them: "It is not for you to know the times or dates the Father has set by his own authority. But you will receive power when the Holy Spirit comes on you; and you will be my witnesses in Jerusalem, and in all Judea and Samaria, and to the ends of the earth." After he said this, he was taken up before their very eyes, and a cloud hid him from their sight. They were looking intently up into the sky as he was going, when suddenly two men dressed in white stood beside them.

The writer of Acts is the same person who wrote the Gospel of Luke. At the very end of that gospel, he says that the event took place in Bethany. But in Acts, it appears that it took place on the Mount of Olives. It was there, when Christians began to celebrate the Ascension as a special feast day toward the end of the fourth century, that a basilica was built to commemorate the spot. As an interesting sidebar, the site was acquired by emissaries of the Muslim crusading hero, Saladin, and has remained under the control of the Islamic *Waqf* ever since.[9]

When did the ascension take place? Acts says that Jesus was taken up forty days after the resurrection. Marcus Borg suggests reading the forty days in Acts metaphorically, meaning after a long time.[10] But in his gospel, if one follows the sequence of events carefully, Luke seems to say that it happened on the evening of the day after the resurrection. A day and a half is hardly enough time to squeeze in all of the post-resurrection appearances of Jesus

8. Wright, Surprised by Hope, 109–17.
9. http://en.wikipedia.org/wiki/Ascension_of_Jesus # Location.
10. Marcus Borg. "The Ascension of Jesus," http:www.beliefnet.com/Faiths/Christianity/2000/05/ The-Ascension-Of-Jesus.aspx?www.beliefnet.com/Faiths/Christianity/2000/05/The-Ascension-Of-Jesus.aspx?

that we read about in scripture. On the other hand, it is not unusual for
Biblical writers to compress or collapse a number of events into a much
shorter narrative.

Luke tells us both in his gospel and in Acts that Jesus "was taken up." The
passive voice, that Jesus was taken up, is confirmed in Mark 16:19–20 and
is echoed in Quran 3:55, "God said, 'O Jesus, I will raise thee to Myself.'"
But where did Jesus go? Luke and John say "to heaven," and the direction
that Jesus went was upward. Are these references of "upward" and "heaven"
metaphor for the traditional tripartite view of heaven, earth, and hell being
in vertical relationship with hell being below the earth and heaven being
above? Both Christian and Muslim texts imply that the ascension was in the
flesh, that is, Jesus' body was raised up. Tradition in both faiths seems to
support that. So, where did Jesus' body go and, more importantly, where is
it now? N.T. Wright would also say "to heaven." But he would go on to say
that "heaven and earth in biblical cosmology are not two different locations
within the same continuum of space and matter. They are two different
dimensions of God's good creation." Still further, he says that "heaven is, as it
were, the control room for earth; it is the CEO's office, the place from which
instructions are given. 'All authority is given to me,' said Jesus at the end of
Matthew's gospel, 'in heaven and on earth.'"[11] Wright assures us that Jesus is
in both places, heaven and earth. He is corporally in heaven *at the right hand*
of God—somehow elevated to the same status as God in the CEO's office.
And, in this case, heaven is not a metaphor but rather a mystery, a different
kind of space and matter than earth.

Christians believe that, in another sense, Jesus remains with them/us on
earth. That is the role of the Holy Spirit. In the passage of Acts cited above,
Jesus promises his disciples that they will receive the power of the Holy Spirit
so they can go forth to be Jesus' witnesses. John 20:21–23 confirms that
promise: "'as the Father has sent me, I also send you.' And when he had said
this, he breathed on them and said to them, 'Receive the Holy Spirit.'" In
saying this, Jesus is clearly acting as God. The Quran does not place these
words in Jesus' mouth, but it does place them in the mouth of God. "When
I have fashioned him [man] and breathed into him My spirit..." (Quran
15:29). The spirit of God expressed here refers to those God-like qualities
such as knowledge and free will, the soul given by God to all humans.

Christians believe that Jesus remains with them here on earth through the
indwelling of the Holy Spirit. This makes sense only within the framework of
trinitarian theology where we can expect some disagreement between the two
faiths, a topic we will take up in the next chapter.

11. Wright, *Surprised by Hope*, 111.

One thing that most Christians *and* most Muslims do agree on is that the combination of the resurrection and ascension, or just the ascension (if one doesn't believe in the resurrection), is that they manifest Jesus' triumph over death, over those evil forces in the world that conspire against him and what his life represents. In Quran 3:55, God continues beyond what we quoted at the beginning of the chapter: "...and clear thee of the falsehoods of those who blaspheme; I will make those who follow thee superior to those who reject faith, to the Day of Resurrection."

In a small book, *The Islamic Jesus*, Daniel Deleanu makes a monumental statement in reference to Quran 4:157, "They did not kill Him, they did not crucify Him, it only seemed to them to be so." Deleanu says that "This affirmation points out the 'illusory' death, not in the sense that He did not die on the cross, but in the sense that His death means resurrection and life." When the Quran says that "but they killed him not nor crucified him," it means that the plan of terminating Jesus was unsuccessful.[12]

One day, Deleanu's book in hand, I discussed this idea with brother Nahidian, imam of the mosque in Manassas, Virginia. Brother Nahidian did not quite see it that way; he held to the idea that Jesus was not crucified. But he did agree that the death of Jesus is surrounded by as much mystery as his birth. And that more important than whether or not he was crucified is his being taken up to heaven in glory, and his coming back again to lead us all to judgment—his ultimate triumph over evil itself, over attempts to kill him, over death itself. This thought is echoed by a well-known contemporary Muslim writer, Tarif Khalidi, who says: "It is the Ascension rather than the Crucifixion which marks the high point of his life in the Quran and in the Muslim tradition as a whole."[13]

Although it is true that many, and maybe even most, Muslims believe that someone other than Jesus was actually nailed to the cross, we have seen that there are some Muslims who do believe that it was actually Jesus who was crucified. Let's return for a moment to the reference to the Brethren of Purity who wrote, "Jesus' humanity was crucified and his hands were nailed to the cross. He was left there all day, given vinegar to drink, and pierced with a lance. He was taken down from the cross, wrapped in a shroud and laid in a tomb. Three days later, he appeared to the disciples and was recognized by them."[14] Not only does this text profess a belief in the crucifixion, but it also describes one post-resurrection appearance of Jesus.

12. Daniel Deleanu, *The Islamic Jesus: The Portrait of Jesus in Islamic Literature and Tradition* (Lincoln, NB: Writers Club Press, 2002), xix.

13. Tarif Khalidi, *The Muslim Jesus: Sayings and Stories in Islamic Literature* (Cambridge, MA and London: Harvard University Press, 2001), 13.

14. Robinson, *Christ in Islam*, 57.

The medieval Islamic writer Ibn al-Athir also reports an Islamic tradition whereby Jesus was taken up to heaven in the flesh, just as the ascension is described in Christian scripture. Seven days later, he returned to earth. He appeared first to his mother Mary who was still weeping for him. She then gathered the disciples to him and he commissioned them to go forth with the message that God had given him. Then God raised Jesus to heaven once again, and the disciples did as Jesus commanded. "The Messiah's raising up was three hundred and thirty-six years after Alexander's conquest of Darius."[15] The battle that the text refers to took place in 331 BC. So, the number of years does not correspond exactly with the New Testament narratives, but it does fit within the time frame of Jesus' historical life here on earth. The important point here is that there are, or at least were, some Muslims who believe that Jesus died, was raised from the dead, appeared to his disciples and bestowed on them the great commission to go out to preach the word of God as he presented it, and then ascended to heaven from where he will come at the end of time on the day of judgment.

Another issue on which Christian and Muslim scriptures converge is on what will happen next. The statement regarding this issue, made by my former Vanderbilt student Parwana, really took me by surprise. You will recall my reference to her and her statement in the introduction. She said:

> I find His (Jesus') contribution to Muslim beliefs to be *underestimated* [emphasis mine]. He was one of the most respected and beloved messengers of God and He is the One who will descend on the Day of Resurrection to lead the Muslims in the world against evil....I find it incredible that it is Jesus, not Muhammad, whom the Muslims will follow during the last days of the world.

She is talking here about the second coming of Jesus.

There are two references in the Quran that point to that second coming. The first is Quran 4:159, just two verses after the Quranic statement about the crucifixion. It says: "And there is none of the People of the Book but must believe in him before his [Jesus'] death; and on the Day of Judgment he will be a witness against them." The second reference is Quran 43:61 which reads: "And Jesus shall be a sign (for the coming of) the Hour (of Judgment): Therefore have no doubt about the (Hour), but follow ye Me: this is a Straight Way." The Quranic term for this event is *yaum al-qiyamah* which most Muslims take to mean the day of judgment and/or the day of resurrection. There are Muslim scholars who point out that neither of these verses specifically says

---

15. Deleanu, *The Islamic Jesus*, 8. See also Parrinder, *Jesus in the Qur'an*, 122.

that Jesus will return to earth.[16] Nor are they specific about what Jesus' role will be at that time. Yet, Abdallah Yusuf Ali's commentary for this verse says, "This is understood to refer to the second coming of Jesus in the Last Days before the Resurrection when he will destroy the false doctrines that pass under his name, and prepare the way for the universal acceptance of Islam, the Gospel of Unity and Peace, the Straight Way of the Quran."

As so often is the case, the details come from *hadith,* traditions of the Prophet. The earliest collection of *hadith,* the *Muwatta,* is silent on Jesus' role in the *yaum al-qiyamah.* But the collections of both al-Bukhari and Sahih Muslim do have a number of traditions that do speak of it. The most specific, considered the most original, and thus the most important says:

> The second agreed upon *hadith* comes from Al-Layth who relates it from Ibn Shihab al-Zuhri who reportedly heard it from Sa'id bin al-Musayyab who in turn heard it from Abu Hurayrah:
> God's Messenger said: By him in whose hands my soul is, (Jesus) son of Mary will descend amongst you shortly as a just ruler (*hakaman muqsitan*) and will break the cross and kill the pig and abolish the *jizyah.* Wealth will flow (in such abundance that) nobody will accept (any charitable gifts) (Bukhari 3/425, Muslim 1/p. 255).[17]

What do Christian scriptures say about all of this? In Matthew 24:27–31, Jesus says:

> "For as lightning that comes from the East is visible even in the West, so will be the coming of the Son of Man. Wherever there is a carcass, there the vultures will gather. Immediately after the distress of those days the sun will be darkened, and the moon will not give its light; the stars will fall from the sky, and the heavenly bodies will be shaken. At that time the sign of the Son of Man will appear in the sky, and all the nations of the earth will mourn. They will see the Son of Man coming on the clouds of the sky, with power and great glory. And he will send his angels with a loud trumpet call, and they will gather his elect from the four winds, from one end of the heavens to the other."

This is Jesus himself speaking. Referring to himself as the "Son of Man," as he often did, Jesus predicts his own return, his own second coming. Although much of the language sounds as if it could be metaphorical, it also sounds like there will some kind of real, physical event. And it will be universal, "from the East...visible to West" and involving "all the nations of the earth."

16. See for example Dr. Ahmad Shafaat's extensive article on this subject, "Islamic View of the Coming/Return of Jesus," http://www.islamicperspectives.com/Return OfJesus.htm.
   17. Ibid., 8.

It will follow a period of turmoil or, as the scripture says, "after the distress of those days." Jesus will be triumphant; he will "send his angels with a loud trumpet call." And he will somehow play the role of judge, "he will gather his elect from the four winds." Acts 10:42 underscores this role as judge: "He commanded us to preach to the people and to testify that he is the one whom God appointed as judge of the living and the dead." The phrase "to judge the living and the dead" is incorporated into the Christian Nicene Creed, somewhat uncomfortably incorporated according to N.T. Wright: "The idea that Jesus will come to this world, invading it like a spaceman, smacks to many of an older supernatural or interventionist theology, which they have spent a lifetime rejecting or, at best, reinterpreting."[18] This "judgment," suggests Wright, will not so much be a legalistic, punitive kind of judgment of the world. Rather, it will be God making the world right again, straightening things out, God renewing "the whole cosmos," and somehow "Jesus will be personally present as the center and focus of the new world that will result."[19]

Some Muslims[20] minimize Jesus' role in this event. His role is to announce when the event will take place. But some Muslims, like my student Parwana, see Jesus' role as more. Quran 4:159, at the very least confirms Jesus' presence on the day of judgment/resurrection as he serves as witness for/against those whom God judges among his (Jesus') followers. The *hadith* of al-Bukhari and Sahih Muslim give Jesus another role. He will come as the just ruler, he will break the cross, and kill the pig, and abolish the *jizyah,* the tax paid by Jewish and Christian citizens of a Muslim state.

If, or when, Jesus does abolish the *jizyah*, it will be significant in at least two different ways. First, it would mean equality among Jews, Christians, and Muslims. In earlier times when Islam was expanding, or in Muslim countries where the *jizyah* is collected, people had/have a choice of becoming a Muslim or paying the *jizyah*. The *jizyah* would be abolished if all people were Muslim. Muslims believe that at the second coming, Jesus will return as a Muslim. He will come as a Muslim in the same sense that the Quran says that Abraham is a Muslim: "Abraham was neither a Jew nor a Christian, but a man of pristine faith, a Muslim" (Quran 3:67, Khalidi translation). Let's remember the literal meaning of "Muslim," one who submits to the will of God. On the Mount of Olives, Jesus professed his submission to the will of God (Matthew 26:39, Luke 22:42).

He will break the cross. At first sight, this sounds particularly and specifically anti-Christian. Does it confirm the Muslim denial that Jesus was

---

18. Wright, *Surprised by Hope*, 120.
19. Ibid., 118.
20. Shafaat, "Islamic View of the Coming," 9–10.

crucified? Does it nullify the importance that the cross holds for Christians as a symbol of Christ's sacrifice? Or can Christians, as well as Muslims, find meaning in Jesus breaking the cross? In this latter case, could the breaking of the cross mean something like Jesus' ultimate triumph over the evil in the world that sought to kill him, his ultimate triumph over death itself, or the ultimate triumph over death of all righteous people who, in both Christian and Muslim tradition, will in the end be resurrected from the dead?

There is rarely unanimous agreement on any specific article of faith within each religion, let alone between the two religions. The concept of the resurrection of the dead, the belief that all people will be resurrected at "the end of time," is no different. All three Abrahamic faiths, Judaism, Christianity, and Islam, profess a version of the resurrection of the dead. In ancient Judaism, the Pharisees believed in the literal resurrection of the dead as described in Ezekiel, Chapter 37:

> The hand of the Lord was upon me, and He brought me out by the Spirit of the Lord and set me down in the middle of the valley; and it was full of bones. He caused me to pass among them round about, and behold, *there were* very many on the surface of the valley; and lo, *they were* very dry. He said to me, "Son of man, can these bones live?" And I answered, "O Lord God, You know." Again He said to me, "Prophesy over these bones and say to them, 'O dry bones, hear the word of the Lord.' Thus says the Lord God to these bones, 'Behold, I will cause breath to enter you that you may come to life'…" So I prophesied as He commanded me, and the breath came into them, and they came to life and stood on their feet, an exceedingly great army. Then He said to me, "Son of man, these bones are the whole house of Israel; behold, they say, 'Our bones are dried up and our hope has perished. We are completely cut off.' Therefore prophesy and say to them, 'Thus says the Lord God, Behold, I will open your graves and cause you to come up out of your graves, My people; and I will bring you into the land of Israel.' Then you will know that I am the Lord, when I have opened your graves and caused you to come up out of your graves, My people. I will put My Spirit within you and you will come to life, and I will place you on your own land. Then you will know that I, the Lord, have spoken and done it," declares the Lord. (Ezekiel 37:1–5, 11–14).

The last verses of this passage seem to suggest that these resurrected bones will live on in the promised land. The Book of Daniel says, "Multitudes who sleep in the dust of the earth will awake: some to everlasting life, others to shame and everlasting contempt" (12:2). On the other hand, the twelfth-century Jewish scholar Moses Maimonides, in his thirteen principles of the Jewish Faith, said that this resurrection was not a permanent state. The Sadducees in ancient times rejected the idea of resurrection of the dead altogether. Jesus criticized them for this. All three of the synoptic gospels tell the story of the Sadducees coming to Jesus, trying to catch him in a legalistic dilemma. According to ancient Jewish custom, if a man's married brother died without heirs, he should marry his brother's widow. The Sadducees presented Jesus with the scenario of a man having seven brothers. When the eldest brother died, the next brother married his widow, and so on down to the last surviving brother. So, the widow married each of the seven brothers. The Sadducees asked Jesus which of the seven was the husband of the widow after the resurrection. Jesus answered:

> "When the dead rise, they will neither marry nor be given in marriage; they will be like the angels in heaven. Now about the dead rising—have you not read in the book of Moses, in the account of the bush, how God said to him, 'I am the God of Abraham, the God of Isaac, and the God of Jacob'? He is not the God of the dead, but of the living. You are badly mistaken!" (Mark 12:18–27, Matthew 22:23–33, Luke 20:27–40).

That people will be raised from the dead at the end of times is a central belief in Christianity. It is supported by scripture: "Listen, I tell you a mystery: We will not all sleep, but we will all be changed—in a flash, in the twinkling of an eye, at the last trumpet. For the trumpet will sound, the dead will be raised imperishable, and we will be changed. For the perishable must clothe itself with the imperishable, and the mortal with immortality" (1Cor 15:51–53). And it is incorporated into the Nicene Creed: "On the third day he [Jesus] rose again in accordance with the Scriptures.... We [the rest of humanity who see themselves as God's people] look for the resurrection of the dead, and the life of the world to come." First Jesus, and at the end of times, the rest of us.

Biblical descriptions of the resurrected Jesus describe a body that was *transformed*. It was a body that still showed evidence of the nail wounds in his hands and feet and the wound from the spear thrust into his side, but the wounds were no longer debilitating. To the contrary, they displayed Jesus' triumph over the crucifixion. N.T. Wright suggests that the resurrected bodies of faithful departed will also be transformed as envisaged, says Wright, by C.S. Lewis in The Great Divorce, "bodies that are more solid, more real, more substantial than our present ones."[21] Why these great bodies? Wright says that it is because there will be a lot of work to do, contributing to God's glory in all eternity, being good citizens in God's Kingdom. The bodies will

---

21. Wright, *Surprised by Hope*, 159.

be immortal. They are "a gift of God's grace and love."[22]

The day of resurrection (*yaum al-qiyamah*) is also central to Islam. It is mentioned seventy times in the Quran and countless times in various *hadith* and exegetical writings. This is the event for which Jesus' second coming is a sign. It is the day that all of humanity will be called to judgment, will be called to be accountable for all that they have done, good and bad, throughout their lifetime. Do Muslims believe that all these resurrected bodies will be transformed? The Quran says, "Does man think that We cannot assemble his bones?" God asks. His reply: "Nay We are able to put together in perfect order the very tips of his fingers" (Quran 75:3–4).

But this is judgment day. What comes next? Both Christianity and Islam would agree that some form of reward or punishment comes next. The single most interesting and important artifact that my team excavated in our archaeological work in Sijilmasa, Morocco, is a fragment of wall plaster with three words inscribed on it: *wusaha... kasabat... alayha*. They are three words from Quran 2:286. The entire verse translated reads: "On no soul doth God place a burden greater than it can bear. It gets every good that it earns, and it suffers every ill that it earns," a verse that clearly holds humans responsible for their actions.

I have sometimes heard critics of Islam say that the Muslim God is harsh and arbitrary. Perhaps they are thinking of the theme that is echoed from time to time in the Quran that God chooses whomever he wants to be saved. One such echo is actually in one of my favorite passages, the parable of the light:

> God is the light of the heavens and the earth. His light is like a niche in which is a lantern, the lantern in a glass, the glass like a shimmering star, kindled from a blessed tree, an olive, neither of the East nor of the West, its oil almost aglow, though untouched by fire. Light upon light! *God guides to His light whomever He wills* [emphasis added], God has knowledge of all things (Quran 24:34, Khalidi translation).

Just a few lines further, the same idea is repeated: "And God bestows His bounty, uncountable, upon whomsoever He wills."

It seems logical that an all-powerful God should be able to do that. But it also seems reasonable that an all-merciful God would want to choose everyone except for those who outright reject God. Although I'm sure there are some, I have never met a Muslim who stood in fear of God's arbitrariness on the day of judgment. I was privileged to hear a lecture by the imminent Muslim scholar Suleyman Nyang, who loved to use electronic metaphors to describe

---

22. Ibid., 161.

Muslim articles of faith. This is how Professor Nyang described this final judgment. At birth, Professor Nyang explained, God gave each of us a video recorder. As we go through life, the recorder records absolutely everything we do, *and* everything we think about what we do. On the day of resurrection when we sit down with God, He takes the cassette out of our recorder and places it in His player, and we review the tape together. Then, in his divine mercy, God erases the tape. We should recall that every *sura* of the Quran save one begins with the phrase, "In the name of God, Most Gracious and Most Merciful." The Quran also tells us that Jesus conveyed God's mercy to his followers: "We sent after them [earlier prophets] Jesus the son of Mary, and bestowed on him the Gospel; and We ordained on the hearts of those who followed him compassion and mercy" (Quran 57:27). Jesus is here one of the conduits of God's mercy. We turn next to Jesus' special relationship with God.

CHAPTER EIGHT

I Believe in One God—There Is No God But God

Emmanuel and I were best friends for a long time before he died a few years ago. Among the many memories I have of our relationship are the numerous times we stood together in front of Masaccio's painting in the Church of Santa Maria del Fiore in Florence Italy, the city where Emmanuel grew up, the city we visited together several times during our friendship, and argued about the holy trinity. We could clearly identify God the Father with his majestic beard, dressed in a blue and pink robe, arms outstretched; and God the Son, Jesus Christ, arms outstretched on the cross. But where was the Holy Spirit? Emmanuel would always say: "It's the white dove below the head of God the Father and above the head of Jesus." "No, that's God the Father's shirt collar," was always my retort. Of course, I had no other visible object to point to until I came up with the idea that Masaccio, using an innovative technique called vanishing point, created a three-dimensional sense of space in the vast vault overarching the figures. It was rather clever, I thought, to think of the Holy Spirit as symbolized by the space in the vault. We never resolved the argument. Nor could either of us say that we truly understood the trinity. For sure, neither of us could have explained it to a Muslim.

Nothing could seem more irreconcilable between Christians and Muslims than the doctrine of the trinity and the related doctrine of the incarnation. That there is some ground for agreement, on the other hand, should be obvious since both faiths are adamant about monotheism. Both believe that there is only *one* God. And their scriptures seem to be quite clear about that. About the oneness of God, the Quran is quite clear: "Say not 'Trinity;' desist; it will be better for you, for God is one" (Quran 4:171) a phrase that is echoed over and over again in other verses of the Quran. But it is echoed over and over again in the Bible as well. When one of the teachers of the law asked Jesus what was the most important commandment, Jesus answered: "Here this O Israel, the Lord our God, the Lord is One" (Mark 12:29). But Christian monotheism includes the concept of the trinity—three persons

in one God: Father, Son, and Holy Spirit. The second of the three, Jesus
Christ, is the Son of God, God become man—incarnation. For Muslims,
monotheism is absolute, uncompromising. God is not only *one*, but is not
material, not visible, and most importantly, not divisible.

These are complicated concepts. So complicated, in fact, that they are most
often reduced to rather simple truth statements as we see in the Baltimore
Catechism:

> Question: Is there but one God?
> Answer: Yes; there is but one God.
> Question: Why can there be but one god?
> Answer: There can be but one God because God, being supreme and
> infinite, cannot have an equal.
> Question: How many persons are there in god?
> Answer: In God there are three divine persons really distinct and
> equal in all things—the Father, the Son, and the Holy Spirit.
> Question: Is the Father God?
> Answer: The Father is God and the first Person of the Blessed Trinity.
> Question: Is the Son God?
> Answer: The Son is God and the second Person of the Blessed Trinity.
> Question: Is the Holy Ghost God?
> Answer: The Holy Ghost is God and the third Person of the Blessed
> Trinity.
> Question: What do you mean by the Blessed Trinity?
> Answer: By the Blessed Trinity I mean one God in three Divine
> Persons.
> Question: Are the three Divine Persons equal in all things?
> Answer: The three Divine Persons are equal in all things.
> Question: Are the three Divine Persons one and the same God?
> Answer: The three Divine Persons are one and the same God, having
> one and the same divine nature and substance.
> Question: Can we fully understand how the three Divine Persons are
> one and the same God?
> Answer: We cannot fully understand how the three Divine Persons
> are one and the same God, because this is a mystery.
> Question: What is a mystery?
> Answer: A mystery is a truth which we cannot fully understand.[1]

Faith statements are just as straight forward in Islam. "There is no God but
God, and Muhammad is His prophet" is the first pillar of the faith. Rejection
of the trinity seems quite explicit in the Quran: "They do blaspheme who say:
'God is one of three in a Trinity: for there is no god except One God'"(Quran
5:73). The verse right before that explicitly denies that God is Jesus: "They do

---

1. Kinkead, *Baltimore Catechism*, 39–41.

blaspheme who say: 'God is Christ the son of Mary.'" Muslims also see Quran 3:51, where Jesus states: "It is God who is my Lord and your Lord," as Jesus clearly separating himself from God. That said, the verse is quite similar to the gospel verse where Jesus says, "I am returning to my Father and your Father, to my God and your God" (John 20:17).

The authors of a popular book *Answering Islam*[2] suggest that on several issues, Muslims have misunderstood basic Christian beliefs. They are probably right. But these issues are probably not clearly understood by Christians either. I'm sure I've heard many sermons about the trinity on Trinity Sunday, but I specifically remember two—more accurately, I remember the introductions to two. In the first, the preacher, only half jokingly, pointed out that pastors tend to delegate the task of preaching on Trinity Sunday to an assistant priest or to a visiting preacher. Why? Because the subject is just too difficult. The second introduction to a sermon on the trinity that I remember, by an assistant priest I might add, began by telling the story of a little boy attending Sunday school, when asked by the teacher what the trinity was, he answered with total self assurance, tongue protruding through the gap of his missing two front teeth—"it's a mythtery." He had studied his Baltimore Catechism well. Muslims argue that there *should* be no mystery about the oneness of God.

THE TRINITY IN THE BIBLE
What does the Bible say about the trinity? I was surprised to learn that the word "trinity" does not appear a single time in the Bible. That does not mean that there is not a basis for the concept of trinity in the holy book. The first allusion to the trinity comes right at the beginning of the book, in the first three verses where it says: "In the beginning God created the heavens and the earth. Now the earth was formless and empty, darkness was over the surface of the deep, and the Spirit of God was hovering over the waters. And God said 'Let there be light.'" (Genesis 1:1–3). The first person is associated with the act of creating in verse one. The third person is the Spirit of God in verse two. The second person is the Word of God in verse three. Of course, we have to wait until the New Testament for the Word of God to be identified as Jesus in the Gospel of John, again where it says "In the beginning was the Word, and the Word was with God, and the Word was God" (John 1:1). It is in verse 14 where the Word is said to have become flesh, that is, the incarnation of Jesus.

There is another story in Genesis that may well allude to the trinity. Chapter 18 tells the story of three strangers coming to visit Abraham near the

2. Norman L. Geisler and Abdul Saleeb, *Answering Islam: The Crescent in the Light of the Cross* (Grand Rapids, MI: Baker Books, 2002).

great trees of Mamre. At some point in the encounter, Abraham recognizes
them, or at least one of them, as the Lord God. Some interpreters say that
two of the strangers were angels, but the text itself is very unclear about
this. The three strangers and the Lord seem to be interchangeable. The first
writer to specifically link these three strangers to a sort of trinity was the
first-century Jewish philosopher Philo (30 BC–AD 45). When he interprets
the story of the three stangers' visit to Abraham, he argues that this is an
allegorical presentation of God's *ousia*—He Who is—with his two senior
powers—the Kingly and Creative.[3] During the Middle Ages, iconographers
began to depict the three strangers as the trinity. The most famous of these
was painted sometime between 1411 and 1422 by the Russian iconographer
Andrei Rublev, a monk in the Monastery of the Trinity at Zaforsk. The
original is now in the Tretyakov Gallery in Moscow. Rublev portrays the three
strangers as angels, that is, as belonging to heaven rather that to earth. Their
faces are virtually identical, representing the equality of the three persons of
the trinity. Yet, some sources identify each of the figures respectively as Father,
Son and Holy Spirit.[4]

When we discussed the story of Abraham and the three strangers in my
Jesus in Islam Class at Vanderbilt, one of my Muslim students raised the
question as she observed that the three ate the food offered by Abraham: "If
God were the three visitors, why would God need to eat? I could understand
Jesus, the son possibly eating because of his *human* nature, but why would
God the Father and/or the Holy Spirit need to consume food?" Someone else
observed, "Maybe they didn't *need* to eat. Perhaps we should ask why they
would *want* to eat?" The offering and accepting of hospitality is an integral
part of Middle Eastern culture. It is today and was even more so in the time

3. Karen Armstrong, *A History of God: The 4,000-Year Quest of Judaism, Christianity, and Islam*
(New York: Alfred A. Knopf, 1993), 68–69.
4. http://www.printeryhouse.org/icons/C03.asp.

of Abraham. If these strangers did indeed somehow represent God, and God has the infinite power to do whatever, would they not have *wanted* to accept Abraham's hospitality?

It is in the New Testament that we should expect to find more specific references to the holy trinity. In the story of Jesus' baptism by John the Baptist, we are told that Jesus came up out of the water and "saw the Spirit of God descending like a dove and lighting on him. And a voice from heaven said, 'This is my Son...'" (Matthew 3:16–17). So, Jesus and the Holy Spirit are seen together, and God the Father is heard. A little further in Matthew, Jesus commands his apostles to go out and baptize "in the name of the Father, and of the Son, and of the Holy Spirit." (Matt. 28:19). All three persons of the trinity are specifically identified by name.

Father, Son, and Holy Spirit are also identified by name early on in the Apostles' Creed which, at least according to tradition, dates back to the late first century or second century. One thing to notice here, though, is that God the Father is clearly identified as God, but neither Jesus (who is described as the Son of God) nor the Holy Spirit is specifically identified as God. The development of this trinitarian theology would occur over the next three centuries.

A BRIEF HISTORY OF TRINITARIAN THEOLOGY

During the fourth and fifth centuries of the early Christian era, trinitarianism (the concept of three persons in one God) and Christology (the relationship between Jesus' human and divine natures) were hotly debated issues. So much so that Gregory of Nyssa says of Constantinople as early as the fourth century:

> The city is full of mechanics and slaves who are all of them profound theologians and preach in the shops and the streets. If you want a man to change a piece of silver, he tells you in what way the Son differs from the Father; if you ask the price of a loaf of bread, you are told by way of reply that the Son is inferior to the Father; and if you inquire whether the bath is ready, the answer is that the Son was made of nothing.[5]

There are numerous books that cover this subject during this period. What follows is a brief and hopefully not too oversimplified summary.

Among the heated debates to plague the early church in the late third and early fourth centuries, was what would be called Arianism, named after a priest in Alexandria, Egypt who challenged the view that Jesus Christ, Son

---

5. Quoted in James Westfall Thompson, *An Introduction to Medieval Europe 300–1500* (New York: W.W. Norton and Company, 1937), 41.

of God, *is* God. The teaching actually developed earlier in Antioch and was condemned by three church councils held at Antioch between 264 and 269. The mystery of the incarnation, the idea that Jesus as the Word (*Logos*) of God, as God himself became man, is declared in the Gospel of John: "And the Word became flesh, and dwelt among us, and we saw his glory, glory as of the only begotten from the Father, full of grace and truth" (1:14). The beginning of that chapter in John establishes that Jesus was coeternal with God: "In the beginning was the Word, and the Word was with God, and the Word was God" (1:1). This implies, of course, that Jesus participated in the act of creation. God created through His divine Word. "Then God said, 'Let there be light'" (Genesis 1:3). Classical Greek philosophers also saw the *Logos* as having creative power. The *Logos* is the rational principle that governs and develops the universe, the principle of creation.

The counter argument that Jesus was not there in the beginning was also based on canonical scripture. Proverbs (8:22–31) personifies wisdom as distinct from the Father, begotten by him as his firstborn and as the instrument of creation.

> The Lord brought me [*Logos*] forth as the first of his works,
>   before his deeds of old;
> I was appointed from eternity, from the beginning,
>   before the world began.
> When there were no oceans, I was given birth, when there were no
>   springs abounding with water;
> before the mountains were settled in place, before the hills,
>   I was given birth,
> before he made the earth or its fields or any of the dust of the world.
>   I was there when he set the heavens in place,
>   when he marked out the horizon on the face of the deep,
> when he established the clouds above and
>   fixed securely the fountains of the deep,
> when he gave the sea its boundary so the waters would not overstep
> his command,
>   and when he marked out the foundations of the earth.
> Then I was the craftsman at his side.
> I was filled with delight day after day, rejoicing always in his presence,
>   rejoicing in his whole world and delighting in mankind.

Arius and his followers applied the rules of logic as they read this. In the same way that wisdom was distinct from the Father, Jesus, the Word of God, was also distinct from the Father, begotten at a specific point in time. "God," Arius wrote, "was absolutely one, the only unbegotten, the only eternal, the only one without beginning."[6] He went on to say that "Before he was begotten or created or ordained or established, he [Jesus] did not exist." So, for Arius, the Word had a beginning and was liable to change. Arius's opponents took this as a denial that Jesus *is* God. Most of what we know of Arius we have learned from those opponents. But Arius himself actually may not have gone quite that far. His confessional statement says:

> We believe in one God, the Father, the ruler of all; and in the Lord Jesus Christ, his only Son, the one who was begotten from him before all ages, God the Word, through whom all things came to be, things in the heavens and things on earth; the one who descended and took flesh and suffered and rose and ascended into the heavens and is coming again to judge living and dead. And in the Holy Spirit, and in the resurrection of the flesh and in the life of the age to come and in the Kingdom of the heavens and in [the] one catholic Church of God [extending] from one end of the earth to the other.
>
> We have received this faith from the holy gospels, where the Lord says to his disciples, "go forth and teach all nations, baptizing them in the name of the Father and of the Son and of the Holy Spirit." If we do not believe these things, and if we do not truly accept Father and Son and Holy Spirit just as the whole Catholic Church teaches, and as the Scriptures (which we rely on in all things) teach, God is our judge, now and on the day that is coming...[7]

He seems to be saying that Jesus is *in some way* God, but not in the same way as the Father. Jesus is subsequent to the Father and, therefore, less than the Father.

Arius's chief opponent was his bishop, Athanasius, the same Athanasius whose letter confirmed the canonical Bible. It is interesting that his argument stems from the same passage in Proverbs. Athanasius, referring to Dionysius of Rome, used the phrase "begotten, not made." He argued that "begotten" in this instance means that the Son "is the offspring from the Father's substance... he is the Wisdom (Sophia) and Word (Logos) of the Father."[8] "From the Father's substance" implies that Jesus as Word is not created and shares the Father's eternal existence. His position is stated in the Nicene Creed, adopted at the Council of Nicaea in 325:

> We believe in one God, the Father, the ruler of all, the maker of all

---

6. Arius, *Epistle to Alexander*, quoted in Thomas Bokenkotter, *A Concise History of the Catholic Church* (New York: Doubleday, 2004), 46.

7. Quoted from Rowan Williams, *Arius: Heresy and Tradition* (Grand Rapids, MI: Eerdmans, 2002), 278–79.

8. Athanasius, Orations against the Arians 1.16, cited in Leo D. Lefebure, "The Wisdom of God: Sophia and Christian Theology," *Christian Century*, October 19, 1994.

> things visible and invisible; and in one Lord, Jesus Christ the Son
> of God, begotten as the only Son out of the Father, that is, out of
> the substance of the Father, God from God, light from light, true
> God from true God, begotten, not made, *homousios* with the Father,
> the one through whom all things came to be, things in heaven and
> things in earth, who for us men, and for our salvation, came down
> and was incarnate and was made man; he suffered, and the third day
> he rose again, ascended into heaven;
> from thence he shall come to judge the quick and the dead.
> And in the Holy Ghost....
>
> As for those who say, "there was when he was not," or "he did not
> exist before he was begotten," or "he came into being out of non-
> existence" or who fantasize that the Son of God is [made] from some
> other *hypostasis* or *ousia*, or that he is created or mutable or changeable,
> such people the catholic and apostolic Church anathematizes.[9]

Athanasius's argument is based squarely upon his faith and on his reading
of scripture. Arius is using logical syllogisms as a system of argumentation.
The two men produced two different answers, each one consistent within its
own system of thought. But it was Athanasius's argument that was embodied
in the Nicene Creed and became the dominant position in the church, the
official position, if you will. Some argue that Athanasius carried the day not
so much because of his theology, but rather because he was better positioned
politically at the council.[10]

The first section, "I believe in God the Father, creator of heaven and earth,"
dispenses with God the Father in one simple statement. No argument there.
The second section explodes in detail to address several specific problems
of the day. Jesus Christ is described as "God from God, Light from Light,
true God from true God," confirming his divinity. Jesus Christ is said to be
"begotten, not made," that is, coeternal with God the Father, there from the
beginning. Finally, he is said to be "of the substance of the Father," in direct
opposition to Arianism. In 381 the words

> the Lord and Giver of life, who proceedeth from the Father, who
> with the Father and the Son together is worshiped and glorified, who
> spoke by the prophets. In one holy catholic and apostolic Church; we
> acknowledge one baptism for the remission of sins; we look for the
> resurrection of the dead, and the life of the world to come. Amen.

were added to the creed immediately after "And in the Holy Ghost..."

9. Ibid., 278.
10. Richard E. Rubenstein, *When Jesus Became God: The Struggle to Define Christianity during the Last Days of God* (New York: Harcourt, 1999), 68–89.

In the late thirteenth or early fourteenth century, a friar of the third order of St. Francis by the name of Raymond Llull produced a graphic illustration of the trinity as described in the Nicene Creed. Not surprisingly, the trinity was illustrated by a triangle.[11]

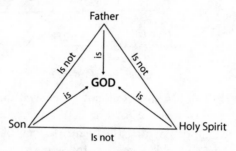

Raymond Lull (cir. 1305)

The triangle is God. Each of the corners represents one of the three persons. Each one is God. The Father is God; the Son is God; and the Holy Spirit is God. But each also has a separate identity. The Father is neither the Son nor the Holy Spirit. The Son is neither the Father nor the Holy Spirit. And the Holy Spirit is neither the Father nor the Son. Incidentally, Llull had a special zeal for explaining Christian concepts to Muslims, albeit for the purpose of converting Muslims to Christianity.

Related to this trinitarian issue is the Christological issue of the relationship between the divinity and the humanity of Jesus.[12] Apollinarius, bishop of Laodicea, in Syria, near Antioch, saw each individual person as made up of three components: a body, a life principle, and a spirit/mind/soul. It is within this last component that the individual's personhood resides. Jesus, in the mind of Apollinarius, is one person who took on a human body and human/animal life principle, but not a human spirit/mind/soul. That remained divine. And since that is where personhood resides, Jesus' person is divine, not human. Apollinarius's view morphed into what would become known as Monophysitism, Jesus was a single divine being who took on some human characteristics. This view can be illustrated with a variant of Llull's diagram. Apollinarius would have placed the "human" circle inside the triangle so that it completely overlapped the "divine" circle.

A little over a quarter of a century later, partly in reaction to Apollinarius, Nestorius, the patriarch of Constantinople, rejected the idea that the Virgin Mary gave birth to God as such. She gave birth to Jesus who was God

11. This illustration, as well as those that follow, is based on illustrations in Geilser and Saleeb, *Answering Islam*, 265–67.

12. My discussion of Christology, unless otherwise referenced, is based on the discussion of this subject in *EFM: Church History*.

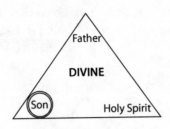

Apollinarious (310–390)

incarnate, but not God. Nestorius's followers pushed this a step further and essentially described Jesus as two persons, one divine with a divine nature and one human with a human nature. The Nestorian view of the trinity might be illustrated by adapting Llull's diagram as follows:

Nestorianism (428–32)

The two circles that represent Jesus are totally separate. One, representing Jesus' divine nature is completely within the triangle. The other circle, the one that represents his human nature, is completely outside the triangle. They do not touch or intersect. According to Nestorius's description, the circles represent two separate persons.

Cyril of Alexandria (412–44) countered Nestorius. He was adamant that Mary was indeed the mother of God, and that God, in the person of Jesus, walked the streets of Nazareth and Jerusalem. Jesus, according to Cyril, has two natures, one divine and one human, that together form one single, inseparable person. At the time of the incarnation, the divine *Logos* (the Word of God) indwelt the man Jesus so fully that the two natures became inseparable. Cyril explained this using an interesting metaphor. Iron, when brought into contact with fire, produces the effects of fire, and fulfils its functions. [13] Jesus the man is like the iron who takes on the properties of the *Logos*, the fire, who dwells within him.

---

13. Cyril of Alexandria, Sermon XXXVI, 7:11, http://www.ccel.org/ccel/pearse/morefathers/files/cyril_on_luke_03_sermons_26_38.htm.

What would become more or less the official position of the Catholic Church was defined at the Council of Chalcedon in 451 in the Creed of Chalcedon:

> We, then, following the holy Fathers, all with one consent, teach men to confess one and the same Son, our Lord Jesus Christ, the same perfect in Godhead and also perfect in manhood; truly God and truly man, of a reasonable [rational] soul and body; consubstantial [co-essential] with the Father according to the Godhead, and consubstantial with us according to the Manhood; in all things like unto us, without sin; begotten before all ages of the Father according to the Godhead, and in these latter days, for us and for our salvation, born of the Virgin Mary, the Mother of God, according to the Manhood; one and the same Christ, Son, Lord, only begotten, to be acknowledged in two natures, inconfusedly, unchangeably, indivisibly, inseparably; the distinction of natures being by no means taken away by the union, but rather the property of each nature being preserved, and concurring in one Person and one Subsistence, not parted or divided into two persons, but one and the same Son, and only begotten, God the Word, the Lord Jesus Christ; as the prophets from the beginning [have declared] concerning Him, and the Lord Jesus Christ Himself has taught us, and the Creed of the holy Fathers has handed down to us.

The creed is quite emphatic. Jesus is one person with two separate natures, one completely human and one completely divine. Jesus is at the same time fully human and fully divine. I can't think of a way to fully illustrate the theology of Chalcedon, but one more adaptation of Llull's diagram might illustrate it as follows:

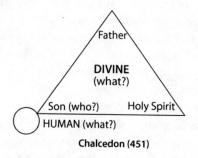

Chalcedon (451)

The circle, Jesus' human nature, is fully outside of the triangle in which his divine nature resides. The circle touches the tip of the triangle to show that the two natures are directly connected to the same one person. So, according to the council's creed, if one asks "who is Jesus?" there is only one answer: "the Son of God." But if one asks "what is Jesus?" the answer is "both human and divine."

WHAT THE BIBLE CLAIMS FOR JESUS

Does the Bible specifically say that Jesus is the Son of God? There are several individuals in the New Testament who refer to Jesus exactly that way. Without providing a complete catalogue, here are a few instances. In the Gospel of Matthew (27:40), those passing by Jesus on the cross taunt him by saying that if he were indeed the Son of God, why does he not save himself and come down from the cross. Apparently, they were among those who thought that Jesus claimed to have been the Son of God. Just a few verses further (Matthew 27:54), the Roman centurion appointed as a guard over the scene of the crucifixion, after seeing everything that had happened, testified that "Surely, he was the Son of God." In Luke, Chapter 4, Jesus is again taunted, this time by the Devil himself saying "If your are the Son of God…" Jesus' response is interesting. He says "Do not put the Lord your God to the test." Is Jesus here saying that he is indeed God Himself? That same question comes up again when Jesus appears on trial before the chief priests and the teachers of the law in Matthew 26 and in Luke 22. The inquisitors ask Jesus if he is the Son of God. He answers "yes I am." Some translations translate the phrase as "You say that I am, but I say…" and Jesus goes on to identify himself as the Son of man. The Greek text supports the latter translation. This is somewhat ambiguous. Is Jesus agreeing with them or not? The Gospel of Mark (14: 62) seems to clear this up; the Greek text as well as all English translations support Jesus answering the question "I am." There is at least one instance in the Gospel of John where Jesus seems to be identifying himself as God. On one occasion as he was talking to a group of Jews who were out to get him; they assured him that they were faithful descendants of Abraham. More than that, Jesus said, "I tell you the truth, before Abraham was born, I am" (John 8:58). The phrase "I am" is the same phrase that God used to identify himself to Moses in Exodus. Judging by their reaction, the crowd seemed to think that by using that phrase, Jesus claimed to be God.

In the New Testament, Jesus is often referred to—indeed, Jesus often referred to himself—as "Son of man," a phrase that appears many times in both the Old and New Testaments. The most common use of the term in both Hebrew and Aramaic is "human." That's what it means in early Semitic literature as well as in the Hebrew Bible. It is arguably what it also means in the New Testament, although some scholars argue that it takes on a Messianic significance as it applies to Jesus himself. But even as it applies to Jesus, it doesn't have to mean anything other than human. It underscores the human quality of Jesus, something that both Christians and Muslims agree on.

Just how human was Jesus? Fully human. I think all Muslims and most Christians would agree on that. The concept of *kenosis* (emptying), as described in Philippians 2:6–8, sheds some light on the Christian understanding of Jesus' humanity: "Who, being in very nature God, did not consider equality with God something to be grasped, but made himself nothing [emptied himself of his divine attributes], taking the very nature of a servant, being made in human likeness. And being found in appearance as a man, he humbled himself and became obedient to death—even death on a cross!" Many Christians believe that, during the period that Jesus lived on earth as a human, he suspended his divine attributes including that of being all-knowing: "No one knows about that day or hour, not even the angels in heaven, nor the Son, but only the Father" (Matthew 24:36). Being fully human during his stay here on earth would explain why he attributed his miracles to God as we saw in Chapter Four, why he submitted to the will of God, why he felt abandoned by God when he was on the cross.

The novel as a literary genre gives one a little more freedom to express ideas that are otherwise difficult to articulate. So, too, it might lend freedom to articulate thoughts about the nature of Jesus. This is the case with William P. Young's novel, *The Shack*. The story is about Mackenzie Allen Phillips, Mack to his wife and very closest friends, who, after experiencing the gut-wrenching tragedy of loosing his youngest daughter to a brutal murder, spends a weekend in the shack that was the scene of the murder with God. At one point, Mack expresses his anger and lashes out at God:

> "At the cross? Now wait, I thought you *left* him [Jesus]—you know—'My God, my god, why hast thou forsaken me?'" It was a Scripture that had often haunted Mack in *The Great Sadness* [what he called his state of depression].
>
> "You misunderstand the mystery there. Regardless of what he felt at that moment, I never left him."
>
> "How can you say that? You abandoned him just like you abandoned me!"
>
> "Mackenzie, I never left him, and I have never left you."
>
> "That makes no sense to me," he snapped.
>
> "I know it doesn't, at least not yet. Will you at least consider this: When all you can see is your pain, perhaps then you lose sight of me?"[14]

14. William P. Young, *The Shack* (Newberry Park, CA: Windblown Media, 2007), 96.

Jesus was so fully human and so full of pain, that he, for a moment, lost sight of God.

About the oneness of God, the Quran is quite clear: "Say not 'Trinity;' desist; it will be better for you, for God is one" (Quran 4:171) a phrase that is echoed over and over again in other verses of the Quran. One of the echoes of Quran verse 4:171 quoted above is 112:1–4:

> Say: He is God the One and Only;
> God the Eternal Absolute;
> He begetteth not nor is He begotten;
> And there is none like unto Him.

The rub comes in the third verse: God "begetteth not nor is He begotten." The problem is with the meaning of the world "beget." Muslims do not, indeed cannot accept the idea of God engaging in the act of begetting. Quran 112:3 is a direct rejection of the idea of God begetting in the very literal, physical, biological, DNA sense of the word. Do Christians use the term "beget" in a literal, physical, biological, DNA sense of the word? I think most would say no.

Not only do Muslims reject the idea of God begetting, they reject the very idea of there being gods other than God. There is another verse that is very revealing:

> Have ye seen Lat and Uzza
> And another the third (goddess) Manat?
> What! For you the male sex and for Him the female?
> Behold such would be indeed a division most unfair.

The three names in those verses refer to the *banat* Allah, the daughters of god. There was a sense of a main god in pre-Islamic Arabia, and he was called Allah. The Quran suggests that he was known to the pre-Islamic Arabs, possibly as the supreme deity and certainly as a creator-god. He was one of the Meccan deities,[15] and he had three daughters: al-Lat (the feminine form of Allah which could be translated as "goddess"), al-Uzza, and Manat.[16] Some early Arab historians, Ibn Ishaq, al-Tabari, and others, say that Satan inserted a verse between verses 20 and 21, this verse: "these are the exalted *gharaniq* (cranes/intermediaries) whose intercession is to be hoped for" apparently

---

15. *Encyclopaedia of Islam*, 2nd ed. (EI2), vol. I, 402.
16. EI2, vols. V, 693; VI, 373; X, 967.

recognizing the existence of these deities and permitting worshiping them. This latter verse which does not appear in the Quran today, or since the time of Muhammad for that matter, is referred to as the Satanic verse. One story is that Muhammad, who was having a really tough time winning over the Meccans, was tempted by Satan to allow the worship of these goddesses, perhaps thereby making his task that much easier. Without getting into a long discussion of the "Satanic Verses" per se, it is only fair to say that many Muslims reject the notion of this Satanic verse. Their argument is, as we presented in Chapter 2, that the Quran was then as it is now, from the beginning just as God revealed it. Either way, it is quite clear that Muhammad rejected the idea of these three "goddesses" being able to intercede, indeed rejected the very idea that God could beget these three daughters or any other offspring. The Quran itself rejects the idea: "Has then your Lord (O Pagans!) preferred for you sons and taken for Himself daughters among the angels? Truly ye utter a most dreadful saying!" (Quran 17:40). The Muslim revulsion of the very idea of God begetting stems as much from the Satanic Verses, which were seen as pure idolatry, as from any reference to Jesus.

The Quran cautions against the use of the term "Son(s) of God." Quran 9:30 says "The Jews call Uzair (Ezra) a Son of God and the Christians call Christ the Son of God. That is a saying from their mouths; (in this) they but imitate what the unbelievers of old used to say. God's curse be on them: how they are deluded away from the truth!" This is first and foremost a caution of how freely the expression "Son(s) of God" was used by Jews in ancient times. One can find several examples in the Old Testament: "the sons of God saw that the daughters of men were beautiful, and they married any of them they chose" (Genesis 6:2); "When the morning stars sang together and all the sons of God shouted for joy?" (Job 38:7); "Ascribe to the Lord, oh sons of the mighty, ascribe to the Lord glory and strength." (Psalm 29:1). The same caution applies to calling Jesus the Son of God. Are we talking about the literal son in the sense that God engaged in a biological act of engendering Jesus or does "Son" mean a very special connection or relationship between Jesus and God. The Quranic denial of Jesus as Son of God is really a rejection of the notion of divine offspring in the literal physical sense. The twelfth-century Asharite theologian al-Sharastani was willing to accept the identity of Jesus as "the Son of God" if the term were used metaphorically. So was the famous twelfth-century Muslim theologian and mystic al-Ghazzali, reading the Gospel of John. [17] A modern Muslim theologian who is willing to think

17. Leirvik, *Images of Jesus*, 115.

along these lines is Mahmoud Ayoub.[18]

METAPHORS

People sometimes use metaphors to try to describe the trinity. The trinity is like water. It is liquid. But when the temperature goes below 32 degrees Fahrenheit, it becomes solid ice. And when the temperature rises above 212 degrees Fahrenheit, at standard pressure, it turns to steam. Same substance, three different forms. Not bad as a metaphor, but the problem with it is that these three forms do not coexist. The same water cannot be all three at the same time.

Another metaphor I've heard a number of times, most recently from a close friend who is an Episcopal priest, is the man who is at the same time a father, a son, and a husband—one person who functions in three different ways, all at the same time. For me, frankly, this works better than water. But some critics say that this sounds too much like modalism, a heresy that originated in the third century. Sabellius, a Libyan priest, claimed there is only one person in the Godhead, so that the Father, the Son, and the Holy Spirit are all one person with different "offices": God the creator and lawgiver, God the savior, and God the sanctifier, each acting in a different way at a different point in time. The main argument against modalism is that it makes nonsense of Biblical passages where Jesus speaks to the Father (e.g., John 17), or talks about being with the Father (John 14:12, 28, 16:10).[19]

When a Muslim friend came to our home for dinner, as we sat down at the table, we asked God's blessing as is our family's practice. When it is my turn to lead the prayer, I usually say something impromptu rather than something formulaic. This time, I opened the prayer with the words "Heavenly father..." and I immediately sensed discomfort on the part of our Muslim friend. We talked about it afterward. He said that to think about God as father is to think about God in human terms and thus leans toward idolatry. It's not always easy to separate a literal meaning from the metaphor.

Kenneth Bailey talks about this "metaphor" among Middle Eastern Christians. He says right up front that "the warning Islam offers the Christian faith is important for Christians to hear." [20] To think about God solely and literally in human terms could be idolatry. On the other hand, if there is any possible confusion about the meaning of the metaphor, Bailey suggests letting

18. Mahmoud Ayoub, "Jesus the Son of God: A Study of the Terms *Ibn* and *Walad* in the Qur'an and Tafsir Tradition," in Yvonne Yazbeck Haddad and Wadi Z. Haddad, eds., *Christian–Muslim Encounters* (Gainsville: University of Florida Press, 1995), 65–81.

19. http://www.catholic.com/library/God_in_Three_Persons.asp; and http://www.stjohnadulted.org/The_02.htm#Modalism.

20. Bailey, *Jesus*, 99.

Jesus define for himself how he uses the term. Jesus does so, according to Bailey, in the parable of the prodigal son. In that story, "Jesus breaks all bounds of human patriarchy and presents an image that goes far beyond anything his culture expected from any human father."[21] The word for "father" in Aramaic is *abba*, which means not only "father" but also "my father" or "our father." It is the word used to address one's earthly father; but it is also used to address a respected person of rank. The Arabic cognate is *ab*, but it doesn't carry quite the same connotation of reverence or respect. Bailey suggests that when Jesus addressed God as *abba*, "he affirmed a vision of a family of faith that went beyond the community of those who had a racial tie to Abraham.... Thereby if god is 'Our Father,' all people are able to address him equally."[22] To understand the term as Jesus used it, one has to think metaphorically. The terms father and son refer to a very special kind of relationship, a closeness that is difficult for humans to describe except in human terms.

THE PROBLEM WITH LANGUAGE

That the early church struggled so hard for so long in those early centuries of its history suggests just how difficult this issue is: "How to understand God," and "the relationship of Jesus to God." An element that must have contributed to the difficulty is language. The positions in these early centuries of the church were argued in Greek. Trinitarians argued that God was of one essence or one substance; *ousia* is the Greek word that they used. But this one God was understood in three ways, had three "understandings;" *hypostasis* is the Greek word. God is one *ousia* with three *hypostases*. A possible confusion could result here because *hypostasis* can also mean substance, especially when it is translated into Latin *substantia* (literally "to stand under"). *Hypostasis* is also equated to the word *prosopon* (literally "mask," as in drama masks worn on the Greek stage) which we can translate into English as "person." So we end up with an equation that might look something like this:

$$1 \text{ ousia} = 1 \text{ hypostasis} = 1 \text{ substantia} = 1 \text{ substance}$$
$$\text{AND}$$
$$3 \text{ hypostases} = 3 \text{ prosopae} = 3 \text{ personae} = 3 \text{ persons}$$

The eighteenth-century French philosopher Voltaire poked fun at this dilemma when he wrote:

> ...to say that there is but one God, and that, nevertheless, there are three *persons*, each of which is truly God; that this distinction, of

21. Ibid.
22. Ibid., 96.

one in *essence*, and *three* in *person*, was never in Scripture; that it is manifestly false, since it is certain that there are no fewer essences than persons, nor persons than essences; that the three persons of the Trinity are either three different substances, or accidents of the divine essence, or that essence itself without distinction; that, in the first place, you make three Gods; that, in the second, God is composed of accidents; you adore accidents, and metamorphose accidents into persons; that, in the third, you unfoundedly and to no purpose divide an indivisible subject, and distinguish into *three* that which within itself has no distinction; that if it be said that the three personalities are neither different substances in the divine essence, nor accidents of that essence, it will be difficult to persuade ourselves that they are anything at all; that it must not be believed that the most rigid and decided Trinitarians have themselves any clear idea of the way in which the three *hypostases* subsist in God, without dividing His substance, and consequently without multiplying it; that St. Augustine himself, after advancing on this subject a thousand reasonings alike dark and false, was forced to confess that nothing intelligible could be said about the matter. [23]

At another level, language can be a problem when it carries a certain amount of cultural baggage. We alluded to this when we discussed the term "beget" earlier. Christians use the term "to beget" in a rather general sense to mean "to cause" or "to produce as an effect." But Muslims see the term in its much more literal sense of physical procreation involving an act that they would find offensive to attribute to God.

MATHEMATICS AS A CULTURALLY NEUTRAL LANGUAGE

Is it possible to find a language that is culturally more neutral? Is mathematics, for example, a culturally neutral language? Geisler and Saleeb offer this intriguing suggestion. What if rather than thinking of the trinity mathematically as addition $(1+1+1=3)$, we thought of it as multiplication $(1 \times 1 \times 1 = 1)$.[24] How exactly does the process of multiplication differ from addition anyway?

One of my students, a brilliant math major, suggested thinking about the trinity in terms of Venn diagrams or Euler diagrams. Shortly thereafter, I found such a diagram representing the trinity on the internet, a thirteenth-century Venn diagram:

23. Voltaire, *A Philosophical Dictionary*, Vol. Iii — Part I.
24. Geisler and Saleeb, *Answering Islam*, 262.

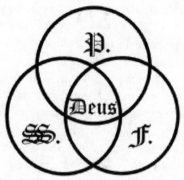

I played around with this idea and came up with one of my own that I think more closely reflects the doctrine as defined at the Council of Chalcedon:

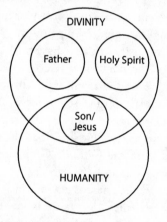

No symbol seems to work perfectly, but here, all three persons are within the one circle representing one divinity. Jesus is also completely within the humanity circle as well.

The mathematical concept of infinity might be helpful in trying to understand God. The famous mathematician, David Hilbert, once wrote: "The infinite! No other question has ever moved so profoundly the spirit of man; no other idea has so fruitfully stimulated his intellect; yet no other concept stands in greater need of clarification than that of the infinite."[25] The Muslim writer Nuh Aydin offers a few examples of mathematical paradoxes based on the principle of infinity. For example, the set of all positive integers (1, 2, 3, 4, 5, 6, etc.) is in a one-to-one correspondence with the set of even positive integers (2, 4, 6, 8, 10, 12, etc.). If this progression went on to infinity, there are as many even positive integers as there are all positive integers. This

25. Quoted in Nuh Aydin, "Infinity: A Window on Divinity," *The Fountain*, 70, July-August, 2009, 39.

would be impossible with finite sets; it is only possible with infinite sets. Nuh Aydin goes on to say that "adding or subtracting one element, or any finite number of elements, from an infinite set does not change its size—or its infiniteness. Adding or subtracting infinitely many elements from an infinite set does not change its size either!"[26] A Christian might want to stop here to conclude that adding (or multiplying) "persons" to God's infinity does not change its size (or unity) either. But Aydin goes on to say that "treating infinity like other numbers (even with the understanding that it is greater than all other numbers) leads to seemingly irresolvable paradoxes. Similarly, treating God like humans leads to an incomplete and incorrect understanding of God and the creation."[27] This is worth exploring more deeply.

INFINITY, TRINITY, AND NINETY-NINE NAMES

On September 11, 2004, the fourth anniversary of the terrorist attack on the World Trade Center, Anglican Archbishop Rowan Williams gave a speech at Al-Azhar Mosque and University in Cairo, Egypt. Much of the speech focused on what he described as "the doctrine of God." I would encourage reading the entire speech which is posted along with all of Archbishop Williams's sermons on the official website of the Archbishop of Canterbury, but here are a few highlights. In this epicenter of Muslim theology, the archbishop began by affirming what Muslims believe. He described the concept of *tawhid* (God is one), and he quoted from the Quran: "God: there is no god but Him, the Ever Living, the Ever Watchful"(Quran 2:255) along with a number of other verses that underscore the oneness of God. He assured his audience that Christians share this same belief, that there is no "disagreement about the nature of God as One and Living and Self-subsistent. For us as for you, it is essential to think of God as a life that has no limit, as a life that is free. God is never to be listed alongside other beings." He referred to several theologians who taught this: "Thomas Aquinas, Ibn Sina, Maimonides, and others." He went on to say that "the true God's freedom is infinite and He can never be limited by any definition. When we have used up all the names that human language can find for Him we shall have spoken true things of Him, but never expressed the whole truth which is hidden from created minds." I can't help but recall my conversation with my friend Whit Bodman about Ibn al-'Arabi's parsing of God's names, many of them in pairs: God the giver of life and God the giver of death, God the all just and God the all merciful, each name in each pair representing an aspect of God that alone is unbalanced. To know God fully, one has to know all of the names. Traditionally, in Islam,

26. Ibid., 40.
27. Ibid., 41.

there are ninety-nine names, but that number is really metaphorical for an infinite number. In fact, if we looked at the various lists of ninety-nine names, there are considerably more than ninety-nine.

Archbishop Williams next sought to clarify some of the things that Christians believe about God. He pointed out that Christians in the first few centuries struggled with the concept of an infinite God and Jesus' relationship to that God. According to those early Christian sages, he said, "when we speak of the Father 'begetting' the Son, we must put out of our minds any suggestion that this is a physical thing, a process like the processes of the world." He went on to say that "the name 'God' is not the name of a person like a human person, a limited being with a father and mother and a place that they inhabit within the world," that "'God' is the name of a kind of life...And that life is lived eternally in three ways which are made known to us in the history of God's revelation to the Hebrew people and in the life of Jesus." He explained that there is a source of Life [God the Father], and expression of life [Jesus], and a sharing of life [the Holy Spirit]. Finally he described how "Christians believe that this life enters ours in a limited degree. When God takes away our evildoing and our guilt, when He forgives us and sets us free, He breathes *new* [emphasis added] life into us, as He breathed life into Adam at first." This breathing of life is the Holy Spirit, the Spirit of God that He breathed into man as described in the Quran (15:29).

SHARING

After all is said and done, what is left that Muslims and Christians can share about their concept of God and about Jesus Christ? About God, they share His unity, His *oneness*. They share a belief that God is infinite, although they explain that infiniteness in different ways—ways neither of which completely capture the infinity of God.

With regard to Jesus, Muslims and Christians can jointly celebrate his humanity. Whatever else Christians believe Jesus to be, all but the ancient Monophysites accept him to be fully human. As for Muslims, they do believe that Jesus was human, only human, but indeed a very special human. Muslims and Christians agree on most of the historical events in Jesus' life, albeit there are problems of interpretation concerning the crucifixion. Most agree on his virgin birth, on his miracles, on his being empowered by the Spirit of God, and on calling him "the Word of God." The Quran itself describes Jesus as "the Word of God" (Quran 4:171). Most Muslims do not understand this to mean that Jesus was present in all eternity or at the time of creation as described in the Book of Genesis as we saw at the beginning of this chapter. But one could read the Quran as saying that the Word became flesh. At the time of the annunciation,

> Behold! the angels said "O Mary! God giveth thee glad
> tidings of a Word from Him: his name will be Christ Jesus the son
> of Mary held in honor in this world and the Hereafter and of (the
> company of) those nearest to God. He shall speak to the people in
> childhood and in maturity and he shall be (of the company) of the
> righteous." She said: "O my Lord! how shall I have a son when no
> man hath touched me?" He said: "Even so: God createth what He
> willeth; when He hath decreed a plan He but saith to it 'Be' and
> it is! And God will teach him the Book and Wisdom the Law and
> the Gospel. And (appoint him) an Apostle to the Children of Israel
> (with this message): I have come to you with a sign from your Lord
> in that I make for you out of clay as it were the figure of a bird and
> breathe into it and it becomes a bird by God's leave; and I heal those
> born blind and the lepers and I quicken the dead by God's leave; and
> I declare to you what you eat and what you store in your houses.
> Surely therein is a Sign for you if you did believe" (Quran 3:45–49).

Jesus is a sign of the creative power of God. The Quran describes a miracle, creating birds of clay and breathing life into them, which he will perform through Jesus. That Jesus is Christ—the Messiah, the anointed one—is attested eleven times in the Quran. That Jesus is empowered by the Holy Spirit is stated in Quran 2:87: "We gave Jesus the son of Mary clear (Signs) and strengthened him with the Holy Spirit," that is, the Spirit of God, again identified by some Muslim exegetes as Gabriel.

The rub comes with the Christian belief that Jesus, in addition to being fully human, is also God. No Muslim would ever proclaim that as an absolute faith statement. In fact, they would declare exactly the opposite as an absolute faith statement. But for the sake of dialogue, let's, just for a moment, back away from absolute faith statements. Instead of asking whether or not Jesus is God, let's ask the question in a different way: "does Jesus have to be God?" Many Christians would answer yes, because only a human sacrifice can atone for human sin. We have already dealt with the issue of atonement in an earlier chapter. We have nothing to add to that discussion here. Deitrich Bonhoeffer says that Jesus had to be divine in order to be completely free from self: "He was free from anxiety and the need to establish his own identity, but he was above all free for his neighbor. This was the characteristic which Bonhoeffer, in his last writings, found so impressive. He was free to be compassionate for his neighbor, whoever that neighbor might be, without regard to himself."[28] Could just a normal human be that free? Only God could be that free.

28. *EFM (Education for Ministry) Year Four: Theological Choices,* 5th ed. (Sewanee, TN: The University of the South, 2002, revised in 2004 and 2006), 432.

I wonder, having a flashback to the similar discussion we had in my Introduction to Islam class about the Old Testament trinity, about why the three strangers who came to visit Abraham might *want* to eat, what the answer might be if we asked the question in a slightly different way: "why would God *want* to be human?"—assuming, again, that God can do whatever He wants.

We have already considered in Chapter One that God wants to become manifest, wants to have a relationship with His creation. There is a literary device that figures in the folklore of many cultures. The king goes in disguise among his subjects to learn what they are thinking. A classic example is King Henry V in Shakespeare's play; he goes in disguise among his common soldiers on the eve of the Battle of Agincourt to learn what they are thinking about the impending battle. In 1979, the *Pittsburg Post-Gazette* suggested a similar scenario about President Jimmy Carter who made a surprise visit with the William Fishers of Carnegie on the eve of his Sunday night address to the nation on energy. A surprisingly touching story comes from the writing of American author Mark Twain. In *A Connecticut Yankee in King Arthur's Court*, King Arthur travels with the Connecticut Yankee, both of them disguised as peasants. They come upon a small peasant hut. The father of the household lies dead of smallpox, and the wife tries to turn away the two travelers. The king refuses and, in fact, climbs to the loft to check on their sick child. Then, the Yankee is struck by what he saw:

> There was a slight noise from the direction of the dim corner where the ladder was. It was the king descending. I could see that he was bearing something in one arm, and assisting himself with the other. He came forward into the light; upon his breast lay a slender girl of fifteen. She was but half conscious; she was dying of smallpox. Here was heroism at its last and loftiest possibility, its utmost summit; this was challenging death in the open field unarmed, with all the odds against the challenger, no reward set upon the contest, and no admiring world in silks and cloth of gold to gaze and applaud; and yet the king's bearing was as serenely brave as it had always been in those cheaper contests where knight meets knight in equal fight and clothed in protecting steel. He was great now; sublimely great. The rude statues of his ancestors in his palace should have an addition—I would see to that; and it would not be a mailed king killing a giant or a dragon, like the rest. It would be a king in commoner's garb bearing death in his arms.

This story resonates for some Christians. Of course, God would not *need* to become like us to know what we are thinking or what we are like, but He might *want* to in order for us to more readily interact with Him. At least one

Christian commentator sees a Christ figure in this story.[29]

Whereas a Muslim probably would not raise this question, a Christian might ask: "*In what way* is/could Jesus be divine?" Late eighteenth-early nineteenth-century philosopher/theologian, Friedrich Schleiermacher, says that, in the person of Jesus, "human God-consciousness appears in its perfect archetypal form."[30] Implicit in this statement is the affirmation that Jesus is the fulfillment of human nature. "God-consciousness appearing in an actual human life is the historical fulfillment of the potentiality promised in original perfection. Implicit also is a claim to the sinlessness of Jesus, since perfect God-consciousness means the total absence of sin-consciousness."[31] In other words, Jesus is the perfect human. He is sinless. So he was before his historical birth, and so he remains after his historical death.

Muslims, too, believe that Jesus was sinless. When the angel announced to Mary the birth of her son, he said: "Nay I am only a messenger from thy Lord (to announce) to thee the gift of a holy son" (Quran 19:19). The Pickthall translation of the Quran says "faultless son," and the new Tarif Khalidi translation says "son most pure." All other humans, except arguably the Virgin Mary and John the Baptist,[32] have sinned, even the prophet Muhammad. Addressing Muhammad, God says: "Know therefore that there is no god but God and ask forgiveness for thy fault" (Quran 47:19). Abdallah Yusuf Ali's note to a similar verse explains that "Every mortal according to his nature and degree of spiritual enlightenment falls short of the perfect standard of God, and should therefore ask God for forgiveness."[33]

Muslims believe in the concept of "the perfect man," *al-Insan al-Kamil* in Arabic. The famous twelfth-century Muslim theologian, al-Ghazzali, began to articulate a concept of human correspondence with God. But it is Ibn al-'Arabi who developed in detail the idea of *al-Insan al-Kamil*. The "perfect man" is "the mystic who is perfected, not in an ethical sense, but as encompassing all of God's attributes. Such a man unites God with the world, not as a bridge, but as an interface (*barzakh*)."[34] If Muslims identify any

---

29. http://www.creativeyouthideas.com/blog/teaching_illustrations/the_king_bearing_us_in_his_arms.html.

30. EFM, *Theological Choices*, 83.

31. Ibid.

32. Just as Catholics believe that Mary was born without sin (the Immaculate Conception), some Muslims also believe this based on the verses in the Quran 3:36–37: "And I commend her and her offspring to thy protection from Satan the rejected. Right graciously did her Lord accept her: He made her grow in purity and beauty." As for John the Baptist, "We gave him wisdom even as a youth and pity (for all creatures) as from Us and purity" (Quran 19:12–13).

33. Note to Quran 40:55: "Patiently then persevere: for the Promise of Allah is true: and ask forgiveness for thy fault and celebrate the Praises of thy Lord in the evening and in the morning."

34. Julian Baldick, *Mystical Islam: An Introduction to Sufism* (New York: New York University Press, 2000), 84.

human as "the perfect man," as Ibn al-'Arabi did, they usually say it is the Prophet Muhammad. In this context, Muhammad is more of an archetypal figure than a person. Some Sufis choose not to identify who the "perfect man" is. Could it be Jesus? When I asked my close friend and associate Abdallah this question, he did not reject it out of hand. In fact, he found the whole discussion of *al-Insan al-Kamil* "intriguing." If we are bound by absolute faith statements, the identity of the "perfect man" makes a huge difference. But examining the texture of the concept in Christianity and Islam as it relates to the identity of the infinite God, the concept looks remarkably similar. A graphic depiction might look something like this:

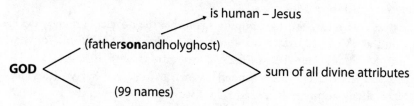

One line, (fathersonandholyghost) represents the trinitarian or Christian approach to describing the infinity of God. God is triune, as opposed to tri-theistic. The three "persons" are somehow distinct but inseparable, like the colors of the rainbow being distinct but inseparable within a single beam of white light. On the other line, the "99 names" of God is the Muslim approach to describing the infinite attributes of God. What distinguishes the Christian description is the fact that "the Son" is, in some way, God. In the Muslim description, *al-Insan al-Kamil*, as the *perfect human*, in some way, embodies God's attributes as listed in the ninety-nine names. The texture of the Christian and Muslim concepts here is different, but similar.

A GOD WHO IS RELATIONAL

The preacher I described toward the beginning of this chapter, the one who told the story about the little boy with the missing front teeth who explained the trinity as a "mythtery," wrote his masters thesis on the trinity and also published a scholarly paper on the subject entitled "The Promise and Challenge of Trinitarian Spirituality."[35] He discusses a number of issues in this paper, but the single most important point seems to be that the trinitarian God is relational and communal. He writes that "A Trinitarian faith here reminds us that we worship One who is infinite yet triune, sovereign yet free,

---

35. Timothy Jones, "The Promise and Challenge of Trinitarian Spirituality," *Sewanee Theological Review* 46:1 (Christmas 2002), 77–91.

transcendent yet relational, one yet communal."[36] This theme is summed up more simply in Ian Douglas's Trinity Sunday Sermon: "The Trinitarian God is a God whose very essence is defined by relationship." He goes on to say that "being in right relationship, in community, with each other and with creation is the way that we come to experience and participate in the fullness of God." What that means is that God expresses his love within Himself, among the three "persons," and because it is God's very nature to be relational, God chooses to extend that love, share that love outside of Himself among His creation, with *all* of us. Again, it is less a question of God *needing* to share in this way as it is a question of God *wanting* to share, wanting to breath something of Himself into us.

Let us return to *The Shack*, hoping again that the novel as a literary device can find a way to express ideas about the trinity and God's infinity more clearly. Mack, through his intimate conversations with his three hosts—Papa (God the Father), Jesus (under his own name), and Sarayu (the Holy Spirit)—singly and together, gradually discovers who they really are. At one point, "Mack struggled to ask, 'which one of you is God?' 'I am,' said all three in unison."[37]

This next exchange between Mack and Papa is a very interesting description of the trinity:

> "To begin with, that you can't grasp the wonder of my nature is rather a good thing. Who wants to worship a God who can be fully comprehended, eh? Not much mystery in that."
>
> "But what difference does it make that there are three of you, and you are all one God. Did I say that right?"
>
> "Right enough." She grinned. "Mackenzie, it makes all the difference in the world!" She seemed to be enjoying this. "We are not three gods, and we are not talking about one god with three attitudes, like a man who is a husband, father, and worker. I am one God and I am three persons, and each of the three is fully and entirely the one."
>
> The "huh?" Mack had been suppressing finally surfaced in all its glory.
>
> "Never mind that," she continued. "What's important is this: If I were simply One God and only One Person, then you would find yourself in this Creation without something wonderful, without something essential even. And I would be utterly other than I am."
>
> "And we would be without...?" Mack didn't even know how to finish the question.
>
> "Love and relationship. All love and relationship is possible for you only because it already exists within Me, within God myself.

36. Ibid., 83.
37. Young, *The Shack*, 87.

Love is *not* the limitation; love is the flying. I am love."[38]

The reference to flying in this dialogue goes back to something that Jesus said to Mack moments earlier.

> "When *we* [emphasis added; this is not the royal we; when one spoke, it was all three speaking] spoke ourself into human existence as the Son of God, we became fully human. We also chose to embrace all the limitations that this entailed. Even though we have always been present in this created universe, we now became flesh and blood. It would be like this bird, whose nature it is to fly, choosing only to walk and remain grounded. He doesn't stop being the bird, but it does alter his experience of life significantly."[39]

At one point, Mack asks Jesus about the Holy Spirit:

> "Speaking of Sarayu, is she the Holy Spirit?"
> "Yes. She is Creativity; she is Action; she is the Breathing of Life; she is much more. She is *my* Spirit."[40]

A little further on in the story, Jesus explains to Mack that "Sarayu, my Spirit, the Spirit of God" is how he [Jesus] remains or indwells in humans after his death, essentially as it is described in the Gospel of John, Chapter 16.

Muslims, too, believe that Jesus was empowered by the Spirit of God because the Quran tells them so: "We gave Jesus the son of Mary clear (Signs) and strengthened him with the Holy Spirit (*Ruh al-Qudus*)." (2:87). As we have seen earlier, several Muslim exegetes see this Holy Spirit as Gabriel who indwells in Jesus, giving him strength and guidance. In another context, they also believe that this Spirit is the breath of life that God breathed into humankind: "When I have fashioned him (in due proportion) and breathed into him of My spirit (*ruh*), fall ye down in obeisance unto him" (Quran 15:29). Abdallah Yusuf Ali's note to this verse describes God's Spirit to be "the faculty of God-like knowledge and will, which, if rightly used would give man superiority over other creatures." My friend Awadh Binhazim attributes the different levels of meaning of *ruh* to "the richness of the Arabic language." So, whereas Christians and Muslims see the identity of the Holy Spirit as different, they see the *role* of the Holy Spirit as quite similar, that is, to indwell in Jesus and in other righteous humans in order to continue to strengthen and guide them toward judgment day.

There is another character in *The Shack* who adds still another dimension

38. Ibid., 101.
39. Ibid., 99.
40. Ibid., 110, 112.

to understanding God, "a tall, beautiful, olive-skinned woman with chiseled Hispanic features, clothed in a darkly colored flowing robe."[41] Mack was really confused when he first met her, knowing that in his tradition, the Christian tradition, there were *only* three persons in God. Jesus told Mack that her name was Sophia. Mack asked, "But doesn't that make four of you. Is she God too?" Jesus answered, "No Mack, there are only three of us. Sophia is a personification of Papa's [God's] wisdom."[42]

The biblical roots of Sophia go back to the personification of wisdom in the Book of Proverbs, chapter 8. Verses 30 and 31 seem to suggest that Sophia is distinct from God, yet the form in which God approaches humans.[43] Several biblical verses link God's wisdom to his power: Job 9:4, 12:13, 36:5, Daniel 2:20, and Romans 16:25–27. There are numerous references to God's wisdom in the Quran. But one that associates God most directly with both power and wisdom is 39:1: "The revelation of this Book is from God the Exalted in Power Full of Wisdom." At least two of God's ninety-nine names, *al-'alim* (the knower) and *al-hakim* (the wise), confirm that association.

Theologian J. I. Packer divides God's attributes into two categories. Some attributes are incommunicable like God's independence (His oneness), His immutability, His infinity. But then there are other attributes that God intends to communicate or extend to human beings, attributes like freedom (free will), goodness, truth, righteousness, spirituality, *and wisdom*. These latter attributes God possesses to perfection. To the extent to which humans possess these qualities—to a less than perfect extent—humans are created in the image of God,[44] like it says in Genesis 1:26, "Let us make man in Our image, according to Our likeness." Proverbs specifically exhorts humans to seek wisdom: "Wisdom is supreme; therefore get wisdom" (4:7, NIV).

Jesus Christ plays a role in both Christianity and in Islam in communicating wisdom to God's human creation. Quranic verses 43:63–64 assign that role to Jesus: "When Jesus came with Clear Signs he said: 'Now have I come to you with Wisdom and in order to make clear to you some of the (points) on which you dispute: therefore fear God and obey me.'" It was the same Philo of Alexandria who identified the three strangers who visited Abraham as God who, in light of the Gospel of John, also identified Sophia as *Logos*, with the divine in Christ.[45] Paul, in his first letter to the Corinthians specifically identifies Jesus as the wisdom of God: "but to those whom God has called,

41. Ibid., 152.
42. Ibid., 171.
43. Lefebure, "The Wisdom of God."
44. J. I. Packer, *Knowing God* (Downers Grove, IL: InterVarsity Press, 1993), 99–100.
45. Lefebure, "The Wisdom of God."

both Jews and Greeks, Christ the power of God and the wisdom of God"
(1:24, NIV).

One of the definitions of "divine" in Webster's dictionary is "to be
supremely good." If we could say that to be divine is to be X to perfection,
then could we say that Jesus is divine in that he is human to perfection and, as
the perfect human (*al-Insan al-Kamil*) he is fully within the circle of divinity?
I would like to return to the Euler diagram that I drew and presented earlier
to summarize the trinity as defined by the Council of Chalcedon.

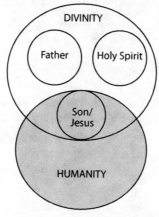

Although diagrams are at best inadequate approximations of the reality
of God, it is only after I looked at this diagram on paper and shaded the
humanity circle that I realized that part of humanity seems to be dragged
into the divinity circle. Could that suggest that humans are invited to share
those communicable attributes of God? Could it also illustrate the role of
Jesus as the perfect human to bring humans, albeit only partly, into God's
circle? Remember Cyril of Alexandria's metaphor of the iron in the fire. Jesus
the man, indwelt by the fire of the divine *Logos*, ignites those who come into
contact with him with that same fire; "so, because it became the flesh of the
Word, Who gives life to all, it therefore also has the power of giving life, and
annihilates the influence of death and corruption."[46]

To go nearly full circle, let's return to the icon of The Old Testament
Trinity painted by the Russian Andrei Rublev.

A priest once described praying as he meditated on the image of the three
heavenly figures seated around the table, reminiscent of the three strangers
who came to Abraham's tent in the Genesis story: "When I pray with it, I
picture God inviting me to the table to join in the fellowship."[47] Surely, this

46. Cyril of Alexandria, Sermon 36.
47. Henry J. M. Nouwen, *Behold the Beauty of the Lord: Praying with Icons* (Notre Dame, IN:
Ave Maria Press, 1987), cited in Jones, "The Promise," 91.

invitation is something that Muslims and Christians could share. As we look at the icon, there is still some space at the front of the table.

More important even than thinking of God as *one* or as *triune* or as having ninety-nine names, perhaps, is thinking of God as *relational*, first and foremost within Himself, and by extension to include us and all of creation. God's triunity is one way of expressing that relationality, and so are God's ninety-nine names, names like "compassionate," "gracious," "nourisher," and so many more, but most important of all, "loving." God is love.

Chapter Nine: Conclusion

In Jesus' Name We Come Together

Love the Lord your God with all your heart and with all your soul
and with all your mind and with all your strength....
Love your neighbor as yourself (Mark 12:30–31).

Those are the two great commandments—in Judaism, Christianity, and Islam!
On the occasion of the Muslim feast of *Eid al-Fitr al-Mubarak*, October 13,
2007, one hundred and thirty-eight Muslim leaders from around the world
addressed an open letter to thirty-two Christian leaders. Here is part of what
they said:

> Whilst Islam and Christianity are obviously different religions—and
> whilst there is no minimizing some of their formal differences—it is
> clear that the *Two Greatest Commandments* are an area of common
> ground and a link between the Quran, the Torah and the New
> Testament. What prefaces the Two Commandments in the Torah
> and the New Testament, and what they arise out of, is the Unity
> of God—that there is only one God...Thus the Unity of God, *love*
> [emphasis mine], and love of the neighbour form a common ground
> upon which Islam and Christianity [and Judaism] are founded.
>   This could not be otherwise since Jesus said: (Matthew 22:40)
> "*On these two commandments hang all the Law and the Prophets.*"

More than once I have heard someone say that one of the main differences
between Islam and Christianity is love. Christianity is a religion of love. But
love, God's love for man as well as man's love for God, seems to be missing
in Islam. When I tell my Muslim friends this, they are puzzled. They say that
faith in God goes hand in hand with love of God. The Quran is quite clear
about that: "But those of faith are overflowing in their love for God" (Quran
2:165). What's more, love is one of the seven conditions of the *shahadah*,
the profession of faith. There is a *hadith* that says that Hasan al-Basree said
whoever recites the *shahadah* and fulfills its conditions will enter heaven. The

seventh condition is *marhabah*, love, that is, loving the *shahadah* itself and
loving the people of God (Al-Mujaadilah, 58:22). Saying the profession of
faith doesn't count unless one's life reflects the beliefs, unless one fullfills the
conditions of the faith.

One of my teaching assistants for my Introduction to Islam class, himself
the imam for a local Bosnian–Muslim community, responded by asking if
he could do a lecture in our class about the reciprocal love between God and
humankind. His lecture focused on sufis, Muslim mystics who, in his mind,
seem to epitomize the mutual love between God and man. That's a thought
that is underscored in the textbook we used in class. "The Sufis emphasize
God's love more than his justice, without, of course, denying the latter in any
sense."[1]

One day, my friend Said, a professor from al-Akhawayn University in
Morocco, and I were talking about this book in the making. He said, "I have
to give you a book written by one of my friends, *Jesus in Sufi Tradition*." In
Islam as in Christianity, mystics have an easier time with some issues than
those of us who insist on understanding everything. One thing that I have
learned from the mystics is that it is not necessary to understand everything
about Jesus in order to believe in Jesus. The sufi of sufis, Jalal al-Din Rumi,
equates Jesus with love itself in his verses: "When Jesus, Loves's spirit, takes
flight/ Never again will he lower his wing/ To return to the realm of labor."[2]
In response to one of my Christian friends who claimed a lack of love in
Islam, I did a search in my *'Alim*, a CD version of the Quran, *hadith*, and
commentaries with a powerful search engine. When I searched Abdallah
Yusuf Ali's translation of the Quran and his commentary, there were over
one hundred and fifty hits for the word "love." Here is one that is echoed over
and over again:

> It is not righteousness that ye turn your faces toward East or West;
> but it is righteousness to believe in God and the Last Day and the
> Angels and the Book and the Messengers; to spend of your substance
> out of love for Him, for your kin, for orphans, for the needy, for the
> wayfarer, for those who ask, and for the ransom of slaves (Quran
> 2:177).

And Abdallah Yusuf Ali's note to that verse:

> As if to emphasize again a warning against deadening formalism, we

1. Frederick Mathewson Denny, *An Introduction to Islam*, 2nd ed. (New York: Macmillan
Publishing Company, 1994), 222.
2. Diwan-eshams, quoted from Nurbakhsh 1982, 57 and cited by Leirvik, *Images of Jesus*, 92.

are given a beautiful description of the righteous and God-fearing man. He should obey salutary regulation, but he should fix his gaze on the love of God and the love of his fellow-men.

There is an even larger number of references to love of God and God's love for mankind in the *hadith*. A quick count in *'Alim* yielded over one hundred and seventy-five references. The dominant, recurring theme that runs through all of these quotes is God's two great commandments: love of God and love of neighbor. Here are two of my favorites:

> A bedouin came to the Prophet and said, "O God's Apostle! When will The Hour be established?" The Prophet said, "Wailaka (woe to you), what have you prepared for it?" The bedouin said, "I have not prepared anything for it, except that I love God and His Apostle." The Prophet said, "You will be with those whom you love" (Al-Bukhari 8.188).

> God's Apostle (peace be upon him) said: "A person visited his brother in another town and God deputed an Angel to wait for him on his way and when he came to him he said: 'Where do you intend to go?' He said: 'I intend to go to my brother in this town.' He said: 'Have you done any favor to him (the repayment of which you intend to get)?' He said: 'No, excepting this that I love him for the sake of God, the Exalted and Glorious.' Thereupon he said: 'I am a Messenger to you from God (to inform you) that God loves you as you love your brother for God's sake'" (Sahih Muslim 6226).

Finally, my very favorite story is one narrated by Abu Talib al-Makki (d. 996). One day as Jesus was walking along, he came across a group of worshipers. Jesus asked them why they worshiped. They said out of fear of hell. He then came across another group of worshipers and asked the same question. They answered that they hoped to be rewarded in paradise. Jesus met a third group of worshipers. When he asked who they were, they answered: "We are lovers of God. We worship Him not out of fear of hell or longing for paradise, but out of love for Him and to His greater glory."[3] In both faiths, there seems to be a similar range of reasons to pray.

At a recent conference on the Gülen Movement,[4] I was struck by one of the dominant themes, both of the conference and the movement itself: the connection between pietism and activism, between the acts of worshiping God and doing service. People in the Gülen Movement are really focused on

---

3. Khalidi, *The Muslim Jesus*, 140.
4. "East and West Encounter: The Gülen Movement," University of Southern California, December 4–6, 2009.

service (*hizmet*): education, feeding the hungry, responding to people in crisis in natural disasters, doing essentially what Jesus asks of all his followers. Why this emphasis? The answer is clear and simple, "for the pleasure of God," or "because it is pleasing to God" (*riza-i Ilahi*). Fetullah Gülen, in the spirit of a Sufi mystic, described love as the greatest human power for relating to God and for relating to each other.[5] He said: "Love is the most essential element of every being, and it is the most radiant light, and it is the greatest power; able to resist and overcome all else."[6]

CONNECTING THE DOTS

Christians and Muslims may not connect all of the dots in quite the same way, but open dialogue between them reveals that they share many of the same dots. These are the common dots I have seen as a result of my journey through the writing of this book. Let's start with revelation. Both faiths believe in the same God who wants to make Himself known. Scripture, both in the Bible and the Quran, is quite clear about the identity of this God, the God of Abraham, Isaac, and Jacob (Quran 6:83–84, Acts 3:13). This God makes Himself known through the process of creation. That process accounts for us and for everything else, other than God Himself. God broadcasts an awareness of Himself through His creation and to His creation. God has chosen to facilitate the process by appointing a host of prophets to serve as conduits. For both faiths, Jesus is at the top or near the top of the list of prophets in importance, or near the bottom of the list chronologically, following a long list of Old Testament Prophets. Muslims believe that one final prophet, Muhammad, came after Jesus.

God's manifestation of Himself demands a response. Most Christians and most Muslims believe that we have a choice in how we respond. And for virtually all of us, sooner or later, that response involves sin. Our response, then, invokes a counter response from God. God is chagrined over the sins of the world. He responds both with righteous anger and with mercy. God seeks to restore the relationship that each of us at some point or another breaks. God is a willing partner in the process of restoration. God sends His holy Word to earth to confront the evils of sin. God's Word is a product of His redemptive love.

The scriptures of both faiths refer to Jesus as the *Word of God*, although that means something different in each case. For Christians, the Word became

5. Rev. Loye Ashton, "Defending Religious Diversity and Tolerance in America Today: Lessons from Fethullah Gülen," *Proceedings of Islam in the Contemporary World: The Fethullah Gülen Movement in Thought and Practice*, Rice University, November 12–13, 2005.

6. M. Fethullah Gülen, *Toward a Global Civilization: Love and Tolerance* (Somerset, NJ: The Light, 2006), 32.

flesh (man), and that man is Jesus. Whatever else he may be, Jesus is fully human and, at the same time, the visible image of God. For Muslims, the Word became a book, the Quran, which God sends as a guide for restoring the relationship. Jesus, as the Word of God, is a messenger, a sign, an image, a way to know the God revealed in scripture. Jesus transmitted the word of God like other prophets. Hamid Algar said it this way in one of his lectures, "This word may be equated with Jesus (as) himself, in the sense that Jesus (as) is the bearer of a divine word, of guidance, and insofar as an individual may be identified with the principal purpose for which he is brought into existence, Jesus (as) may be regarded as identical with the divine word which he conveys.[7] We sometimes hear that Muslims consider Jesus to be *just* a prophet. Yes, but a special prophet in a number of ways.

Most Christians, and arguably an even higher percentage of Muslims, believe in the miraculous birth of Jesus, conceived by the Spirit of God, that is, by the command of God and born of the Virgin Mary. There are variants in the story of Jesus' birth between the two faiths as well as within each of the two faiths, but those variants are, for the most part, complementary rather than contradictory.

And Jesus performed miracles, in both scriptures "by my (God's) leave," or "in God's name." Jesus was the perfect servant. He served his fellow man in perfect humility and taught his disciples by example to do the same. Muslims believe that Jesus also created life, "by God's leave," by breathing into birds that he fashioned out of clay.

Not only is Jesus the perfect servant, but living the life of the perfect servant led to his becoming the suffering servant. Even those Muslims who do not believe that Jesus was crucified for the sins of humankind, believe that he was willing to die, that he was persecuted because of the life he led, a life that confronted the evil of sin. They believe that he suffered, if not for us, then at least with us. They believe that his willingness to die, whether he actually died or not, was effective in disarming evil in the world. He makes it possible, or at least easier, for us to confront the evils of sin by following his example to the best of our limited abilities, by sacrificing our lives to the service of God and the service of others.

Mystics have long stressed the notion of imitating Jesus. Most noteworthy is the late medieval Christian mystic, Thomas à Kempis, who wrote the famous tract *The Imitation of Christ*. In modern times, this notion of service to others in imitation of Christ was epitomized by the French monk and missionary, Father Charles de Foucauld. In his earlier life, Charles was a

---

7. Hamid Algar, *Jesus in the Qur'an: His Reality Expounded in the Qur'an* (Oneonta, NY: Islamic Publications International, 1999), 4.

nobleman, heir to a considerable fortune, a trained cavalry officer, and a man who used his fortune to seek all of the pleasures that money could buy. He discovered that these pleasures could not satisfy his desire for happiness. So, he gave it all away. He sought happiness in a relationship with God. He lived as a monk, observing the strictest asceticism among the Tuareg tribes deep in the Sahara desert of Central and Southern Algeria. With whatever he had, he practiced charity toward the Muslim tribesmen among whom he lived, knowing that there was no hope of converting them. That was not his intention. He didn't even try. His purpose was to live a life in imitation of Jesus, and through his own example, to show these Tuareg tribesmen what that kind of life would look like. Among the several biographies of Charles de Foucauld, one of the most touching is by Ali Merad, a Muslim. In a chapter called "Happiness in imitation of Jesus," Merad writes: "the perfect imitation of Jesus by a Christian must assume a great moral and spiritual significance in the eyes of Muslims….Humility, charity, the renunciation of the pleasures and good things of this world and devotion to the service of the poor and unfortunate are virtues that have always strongly impressed Muslims."[8]

In the end, as we saw in Chapter Seven, both faiths believe that Jesus triumphed over death through his resurrection and/or his ascension to God. Christians and Muslims alike await the return of Jesus on judgment day, triumphant over evil and death, to lead the righteous to everlasting life.

CAN CHRISTIANS AND MUSLIMS PRAY TOGETHER?

So, to return to the fundamentally important question raised at the end of the introduction, "Can Christians and Muslims pray together?" I have encountered polar reactions to this question. One position is that it is quite inappropriate or potentially damaging for Christians and Muslims to formulate and celebrate common acts of worship.[9] The reasoning is that when Christians pray, they pray to a triune God: Father, Son, and Holy Spirit, "as instructed by our Lord Jesus." These are terms, according to that position, that would be offensive to Muslims for whom the unity of God is absolute. To omit these terms, from the Christian perspective, would impoverish prayers rather than enrich them. Likewise, this position maintains, we should not expect Muslims to reduce their worship to a point that would be acceptable to Christians. Clearly, this position stresses the differences between the two faiths. In a sense, it is looking at the empty half of the glass that is half full.

The full half of the glass, on the other hand, while recognizing that there

8. Ali Merad, *Christian Hermit in an Islamic World: A Muslim's View of Charles de Foucauld* (Mahwah, NJ: Paulist Press, 1999), 22–23.

9. Alan Wisdom, "Guidelines for Christian-Muslim Dialogue," *Institute on Religion and Democracy,* April 2003.

are differences, stresses the similarities. As Archbishop Rowan Williams expressed so well in his address on September 11, 2004 at Al-Azhar Mosque and University, Christians, too, believe in the absolute unity (i.e., *oneness*) of God. He goes on to say that "it is sad that sometimes an unfaithful or careless Christian way of speaking has led Muslims and Jews to believe that we have a doctrine of God that does not recognize the oneness and sufficiency of God, or that we worship something less than the One, the Eternal."[10] I repeat what I cited earlier of the Archbishop: "There is...a great difference between what I as a Christian must say and what the Muslim will say; but we agree absolutely that God has no need of any other being, and that God is not a mixture or a society of different beings."[11] More important still, according to Archbishop Williams, is the reason it is important to stress the similarities. "To seek to find reconciliation, to refuse revenge and the killing of the innocent, this is a form of adoration toward the One Living and Almighty God."[12] We must recall that the Archbishop gave this talk on the third anniversary of 9/11 when the need for reconciliation was dramatically apparent. In the immediate aftermath of 9/11, there were in fact a number of organized joint prayer services where Christians, Muslims, and Jews did come together to pray for healing, to pray for God's peace.

Is there a prayer that Christians and Muslims could feel comfortable praying together? What about the prayer that Jesus taught his disciples. We can find it in the Gospel of Matthew:

> Pray, then, in this way:
> "Our Father who is in heaven,
> Hallowed be Your name.
> Your kingdom come.
> Your will be done,
> On earth as it is in heaven.
> Give us this day our daily bread.
> And forgive us our debts, as we also have forgiven our debtors.
> And do not lead us into temptation, but deliver us from evil. [For Yours is the kingdom and the power and the glory forever. Amen.]"
> (Matthew 6: 9–13).

I once heard a talk by a Christian missionary who had been working in Egypt. He told this story about one of his very few "converts" to Christianity. It was a woman he heard praying. She was saying a prayer that sounded remarkably

---

10. Rowan Williams, "To Be Worthy of the God We Worship," 9/11 Speech at al-Azhar, http://www.archbishopofcanterbury.org/1943.
11. Ibid.
12. Ibid.

like the Lord's Prayer. He described it to be a miracle. What he did not seem
to know is that there is a tradition of the prophet Muhammad, a *hadit*h, that
teaches Muslims to say "the Lord's Prayer." It goes like this:

> When any one is in suffering, or his brother suffers, then let him pray
> this prayer:
> "Our Lord God who art in heaven, hallowed be Thy name. Thy
> kingdom is in heaven and on earth, and even as the mercy is in
> heaven, so may the mercy also be upon earth. Forgive us our debts
> and our sins, for Thou art the Lord of the good. Send down mercy
> from Thy mercy and healing from Thy healing for those suffering,
> that they may begin to heal (Abu Dawud 3883).

The woman had not really converted to Christianity. She was being very
Muslim as she prayed a prayer common to both faiths. Granted, the prayers
are not exactly the same. One begins by addressing God as "our father," the
other as "Our Lord God." If Christians and Muslims prayed the Lord's prayer
together, whose version would they use? The great French Islamicist, Louis
Massignon, once said: "To understand the other, one does not need to annex
him but to become his guest."[13] A good guest does not go to the host's house
and rearrange the furniture. The suggestion here, I think, is that whoever's
turf they are on should take the lead.

The phrase "our Father" is a stumbling block for Muslims, but is it
insurmountable? Although a Muslim could never address God as "father" in
a literal, biological sense, he might consider thinking about the term "father"
metaphorically as did the twelfth-century Asharite theologian al-Sharastani,
or the more famous twelfth-century theologian al-Ghazzali, or even the
modern Muslim theologian Mahmoud Ayoub. In this case, "father" is not
a biological father. It describes a unique kind of relationship that can not
be fully described except in terms of which humans have some experiential
knowledge, a relationship sort of like a father and a son, but not really. It is
the relationship between the ideal father, a father who loves, protects, and
nurtures and his loving, obedient sons and daughters.

Would the absence of the phrase "our father" irreparably impoverish
the Christian's prayer? Can Christians accept that God's unity in no way
contradicts His tri*unity*? Is the trinitarian paradigm absolutely indispensable,
all of the time? There are, actually, Christians who have trouble applying the
term "father" to God as do Muslims. The medieval mystic Julian of Norwich,
for example, sometimes thought about God as "mother." She wrote:

13. Cited by Zoe Hersov, translator of Ali Merad, *Christian Hermit*, 88.

Just as God is our Father, so God is also our Mother. And He showed me this truth in all things, but especially in those sweet words when He says: "It is I," as if to say, "I am the power and the Goodness of the Father, I am the Wisdom of the Mother, I am the Light and the Grace which is blessed love, I am the Trinity, I am the Unity, I am the supreme Goodness of all kind of things, I am the One who makes you love, I am the One who makes you desire, I am the never-ending fulfilment of all true desires…"

It is thus logical that God, being our Father, be also our Mother. Our Father desires, our Mother operates and our good Lord the Holy Ghost confirms; we are thus well advised to love our God through whom we have our being, to thank him reverently and to praise him for having created us and to pray fervently to our Mother, so as to obtain mercy and compassion, and to pray to our Lord, the Holy Ghost, to obtain help and grace.[14]

In addition, Julian also applies the mother image specifically to Jesus: "A mother can give her child milk to suck, *but our precious mother, Jesus, can feed us with himself.* He does so most courteously and most tenderly, with the Blessed Sacrament, which is the precious food of true life."[15] That image, for her, was more conducive to thinking about Jesus as nurturing.

The modern feminist theologian Sallie McFague cautions against the exclusive use of the trinitarian paradigm (Father, Son, and Holy Spirit) for understanding God. It is one important paradigm, but alone is too limiting. Crossover in either direction would involve having to stop and think about the words, about who God really is—not such a bad thing. Remember what my students agreed on as they were working on the Jesus jigsaw puzzle as described in the introductory chapter. Although we can hope to know enough about God, we will never in this lifetime know everything there is to know. The concept of God is just too big. Praying together would carry with it a willingness to dialogue, to dialogue with self, to dialogue with the other, and possibly to dialogue with the Spirit of God. The payoff might be a richer and fuller understanding of God.

14. Julian of Norwich, *Revelations in Divine Love*, cited in http://www.vatican.va/spirit/documents/spirit_20010807_giuliana-norwich_en.html.
15. Julian of Norwich, *Revelations in Divine Love* (New York: Doubleday, 1977), 192.

WHY?

Muslims and Christians praying together, admittedly, would not be an easy thing to achieve. What would it take to even try? There would have to be a compelling reason. Let's put the notion of praying together aside for a moment. Some people in our church recently talked about having an interfaith progressive dinner, an occasion where we could get together with people of other faiths just to eat, an occasion where we would hope that doctrinal differences would not get in the way of friendly interaction. The question was raised: "Why would we want to do that?" Certainly a fair question. Our outreach committee had just defined the focus of our church's outreach work as "reaching out to families in crisis." The answer to the question that was raised was clear: "Our *global* family is in crisis." I think this is what Archbishop Rowan Williams had in mind when he said: "And if we are committed to this God, we shall be able to do justice and act rightly even when the world around us expects us to follow its own violent ways."16 We are in desperate need to know one another, to respect one another, to love one another as God loves us. So, whatever the cost of reaching out, the proscription of the two great commandments is quite compelling.

If Christians and Muslims prayed together, what would they pray for? A few years ago, a group of my Muslim students did a video on Muslim prayer. In the video, they started with the call to prayer. Then they showed the preparation for prayer, the ritual washing. They demonstrated what the typical prayer was like, all of the prayer positions. The most interesting part of the video was a series of interviews. They went around campus asking several Muslims *why* they prayed. The answers were wide ranging, but nothing really surprising. Many said they prayed in obedience to God; God says that we should pray. They prayed for their families, friends, for good health, success in their work. Some said that they prayed for God's mercy. Some said they prayed out of love for God—a range of reasons that we might expect from any religious population.

Not long ago, some friends and I were talking about the Lord's Prayer. One of my friends thought that it was odd that this be a prayer of petition, for instance, asking God that His will be done. *Of course* God's will will be done. Rather than petition, the Lord's Prayer should be one of affirmation. Kenneth Bailey17 breaks the Lord's Prayer down this way. He says that it presents six petitions to God, the first three of which are focused on God: that God's name be holy, that His kingdom be realized here on earth and in heaven, and that His will be done. The remaining three petitions focus on the

16. Rowan Williams, 9/11 speech.
17. Bailey, *Jesus*, 104–5.

needs of humankind, daily bread, forgiveness in community, and freedom from evil. But then Bailey adds this twist. Those petitions require a response on our part. I am to respect God's holy name; I am to obey the laws of the kingdom; I am to submit to God's will; I must try to be worthy of God's gifts of nourishment; I must forgive those who have hurt me; I must try to live righteously. These, both Christians and Muslims can pray for.

There is, possibly, promise in praying together on yet another level. And this could be the ultimate payoff for praying together. It has to do with the power of group prayer. We had a discussion at our church recently about the meaning of evangelism. This is a term that scares some people. It is also a term for which the meaning is not entirely clear. Does it mean "bringing people *to* Jesus"? Does it mean "bringing people to God *through* Jesus"? Is it the same thing as recruitment, bringing new members into the church?

More literally, evangelism means spreading the "good news," or even better, *sharing* the "good news" of God. When the good news is shared, it is enriched. Christians and Muslims, generally, believe in the power of group prayer. "For where two or three are gathered together in my name, there I am with them" (Matthew 18:20, NIV). Praying in a group somehow enriches the experience. I remember a specific incident that impressed upon me the power of group prayer in Islam. It was in January of 1991, shortly after the beginning of Desert Storm, the US invasion of Iraq. I was watching the nightly news at home in Tennessee at about ten minutes after ten p.m.. The NBC news reporter stationed in Amman, Jordan gave his daily report standing on the same street corner each day, standing in front of a mosque. On this particular day, he said: "Can you hear the *muezzin* (one who calls to prayer) singing the call to prayer in the background?" And yes, there it was, a beautiful, melodic chant resonating in the background: "God is great…I testify that there is no God but God…I testify that Muhammad is the messenger of God…Make haste toward the prayer…Make haste toward the worship…Prayer is better than sleep." This last phrase is chanted only for the early morning prayer. That's when it hit me. I looked at my watch and saw that it was ten after ten p.m.—but not in Amman, Jordan. There, it was ten after six in the morning. Muslims in Amman were saying their *morning* prayer. Muslims in Southeast Asia would have been saying their noontime prayer, and Muslims in California, their nighttime prayer. Around the globe, many millions of Muslims are praying essentially the same prayers, at the same time, facing a common central point—the Kaaba in Mecca. If there is power in group prayer, it is no wonder that Muslims have such a strong sense of community within the *Umma* (brotherhood and sisterhood within Islam). I have observed Muslims praying many times. I have had the privilege of praying with Muslims just a few times: evening prayer occasionally with members of the Muslim Student Association at Middle Tennessee State University whom I served for a while as faculty advisor; in Turkey, a prayer of thanksgiving for a shared meal—*after* dinner which is an interesting twist. Frankly, it was a little awkward at first. It is not something that comes easily; it takes some time to feel close enough to share something as intimate as prayer.

One evening, after a long day of archaeological work, my professional team and I were sitting in the salon of our house waiting for dinner. When it was time for prayer, my Muslim colleagues withdrew to one end of the salon to say their evening prayers. I was the only non-Muslim in the salon. When they were finished, I said how moved I was to hear them pray. One of them, a young man named Montasir, said to me, "why don't you join us tomorrow. The only requirement is that you do the ritual washing beforehand as we do." The ritual washing is really important to Muslims as preparation for prayer. Its purpose is to separate us from our material world and predispose us to be in communion with God. What a wonderful invitation! I was the "guest in their house." But neither they nor I surrendered anything that we fundamentally believe, they as Muslims and I as a Christian. So, we prayed together:

> God is the Greatest!
> Praise and glory be to You, O God.
> Blessed be Your Name, exalted be Your Majesty and Glory.
> There is no God but You.
> I seek God's shelter from Satan, the condemned.
> In the Name of God, the Most Compassionate, the Most Merciful.
> Praise be to God, Lord of the Universe,
> the Most Compassionate, the Most Merciful!
> Master of the Day for Judgment!
> You alone do we worship and You alone do we call on for help.
> Guide us along the Straight Path…

The straight path is the path of the two great commandments, a path that leads to a relationship with God and with our neighbor. If my own experience has taught me anything, it is that the path is easier and so much enriched by a serious, honest dialogue with my Muslim neighbors, within myself, and with God, Lord of the Universe, Most Compassionate, and Most Merciful!

BIBLIOGRAPHY

Algar, Hamid. *Jesus in the Qur'an: His Reality Expounded in the Qur'an*. Oneonta, NY: Islamic Publications International, 1999.

Antier, Jean-Jaques. *Charles de Foucauld (Charles of Jesus)*. San Francisco: Ignatious Press, 1997.

Armstrong, Karen. *A History of God: The 4,000-Year Quest of Judaism, Christianity and Islam*. New York: Alfred A. Knopf, 1993.

_____. *Muhammad: A Biography of the Prophet*. San Francisco: HarperCollins, 1992.

Ashton, Rev. Loye. "Defending Religious Diversity and Tolerance in America Today: Lessons from Fethullah Gülen." *Proceedings of Islam in the Contemporary World: The Fethullah Gülen Movement in Thought and Practice*, Rice University, November 12–13, 2005.

'Ata ur-Rahim, Muhammad. *Jesus: Prophet of Islam*. Elmhurst, NY: Tahrike Tarsile Qur'an, 1996.

Aydin, Nuh. "Infinity: a Window on Divinity." *The Fountain* 70 (July–August, 2009): 39.

Ayoub, Mahmoud. "Towards an Islamic Christology II." *Muslim World* 70 (1980): 101–2.

Bailey, Kenneth. *Jesus through Middle Eastern Eyes*. Dovers Grove, IL: InterVarsity Press, 2008.

Baldick, Julian. *Mystical Islam: An Introduction to Sufism*. New York: New York University Press, 2000.

Barker, Gregory, ed. *Jesus in the World's Faiths*. New York: Orbis Books, 2005.

Basetti-Sani, Julius. "For a Dialogue between Christians and Muslims." *Muslim World* 57 (1967): 130–31.

Bhaktivedanta Swami Prabhupāda, A.C., trans. *Bhāgavata Purāna*, 9.24.34. http://srimadbhagavatam.com/9/24/en.

Bill, James A. and John Alden Williams. *Roman Catholics and Shi'i Muslims: Prayer, Passion, and Politics.* Chapel Hill: University of North Carolina Press, 2002.

Bokenkotter, Thomas. *A Concise History of the Catholic Church.* New York: Doubleday, 1979.

Borg, Marcus. "The Ascension of Jesus." www.beliefnet.com/Faiths/Christianity/2000/05/ The-Ascension-Of-Jesus.aspx?www.beliefnet.com/Faiths/Christianity.

_____. *Meeting Jesus Again for the First Time: The Historical Jesus and the Heart of Contemporary Faith.* San Francisco: HarperCollins, 1994.

_____. *The God We Never Knew: Beyond Dogmatic Religion to more Authentic Contemporary Faith.* San Francisco: HarperCollins, 1997.

Boyd, Dr. Gregory A. and Edward K. *Letters from a Skeptic: A Son Wrestles with His Father's Questions about Christianity.* Colorado Springs: Cook Communications Ministries, 1994.

Brown, Raymond. *An Introduction to New Testament Christology.* New York: Paulist Press, 1994.

Carroll, Warren H. *The Building of Christendom: A History of Christendom*, Vol.2. Front Royal, VA: Christendom College Press, 1987.

Cyril of Alexandria, Sermon XXXVI. http://www.ccel.org/ccel/pearse/morefathers/files/cyril_on_luke_03_sermons_26_38.htm.

Deleanu, Daniel. *The Islamic Jesus: The Portrait of Jesus in Islamic Literature and Tradition.* Lincoln, NB: Writers Club Press, 2002.

Denney, James. *The Death of Christ: Its Place and Interpretation in the Bible.* London: Hodder and Stoughton, 1909

Denny, Frederick Mathewson. *An Introduction to Islam* 2nd ed. New York: Macmillan Publishing Company, 1994.

Edwards, William D., Wesley J. Gabel, Floyd E. Hosmer. "On the Physical Death of Jesus." *Journal of the American Medical Association* 255, no. 11 (March 21, 1986) 1456, cited in T. W. Hunt, *The Mind of Christ.* Nashville: Broadman & Holman Publishers, 1995), 101−2.

EFM (Education for Ministry) Year One: The Old Testament, 3rd ed. Sewanee, TN: The University of the South, 1999, reprinted in 2000 and 2002.

EFM (Education for Ministry) Year Two: The New Testament, 4th ed. Sewanee, TN: The University of the South, 2000.

EFM (Education for Ministry) Year Three: Church History, 4th ed. Sewanee, TN: The University of the South, 2001, revised in 2003 and 2006.

EFM (Education for Ministry) Year Four: Theological Choices, 5th ed. Sewanee, TN: The University of the South, 2002, revised in 2004 and 2006.

Ehrman, Bart D. *Lost Christianities: The Battle for Scripture and the Faiths We Never Knew.* New York: Oxford University Press, 2003.

_____. *Lost Scriptures: The Books that Did Not Make It into the New Testament.* New York: Oxford University Press, 2003.

Forsyth, P.T. *The Cruciality of the Cross.* London: Hodder and Stoughton, 1909.

Geisler, Norman L. and Abdul Saleeb. *Answering Islam: The Crescent in the Light of the Cross.* Grand Rapids, MI: Baker Books, 2001.

Ghazali, Shaykh Muhammad al-. *A Thematic Commentary on the Qur'an.* Herndon, VA: The International Institute of Islamic Thought, 2000.

Greeley, Andrew M. *The Sinai Myth.* Garden City, NY: Doubleday,1972.

Guillaume, A. *The Life of Muhammad: A Translation of Ibn Ishaq's Sirat Rasul Allah.* Oxford: Oxford University Press, 1955.

Gülen, M. Fethullah. *Toward a Global Civilization: Love and Tolerance.* Somerset, NJ: The Light, 2006.

Haddad, Yvonne Yazbeck and Wadi Z. Haddad, eds. *Christian–Muslim Encounters.* Gainsville: University Press of Florida, 1995.

Hunt, T.W. *The Mind of Christ.* Nashville,TN: Broadman and Holman Publishers, 1995.

Hussein, Muhammad Kamel. *The City of Wrong: A Friday in Jerusalem.* Translated by Kenneth Cragg. Oxford: Oneworld, 1994.

Ibn Kathir. *Tafsir Ibn Kathir,* Abridged, Vol. 7. Riyad: Darussalam Publishers and Distributors, 2000.

Jeffery, Arthur. *The Foreign Vocabulary of the Qur'an.* Boston: Brill, 2006.

Jones, Timothy. "The Promise and Challenge of Trinitarian Spirituality," *Sewanee Theological Review* 46 (Christmas 2002): 77–91.

Julian of Norwich. *Revelations in Divine Love.* New York: Doubleday, 1977.

Kasser, Rodolphe, Marvin Meyer, and Gregor Wurst, eds. *The Gospel of Judas.* National Geographic, 2006.

Khalidi, Tarif. *The Muslim Jesus: Sayings and Stories in Islamic Literature.* Cambridge, MA and London: Harvard University Press, 2001.

_____. *The Qur'an: A New Translation*. New York: Viking, 2008.

Kimball, Charles. *Striving Together: A Way Forward in Christian-Muslim Relations*. Maryknoll, NY: Orbis Books, 1991.

Kinkead, Thomas L. *An Explanation of the Baltimore Catechism of Christian Doctrine*. Rockford, IL: Tan Books and Publishers, 1988.

Kuhn, Thomas S. *The Structure of Scientific Revolutions*, 3rd ed. Chicago: University of Chicago Press, 1996.

Lawson, Benjamin Todd. "The Crucifixion of Jesus in the Qur'an and Qur'anic Commentary: A Historical Survey," Part I. *The Bulletin of the Henry Martyn Institute of Islamic Studies* 10, issue 2 (April–June, 1991): 34–62; Part II, issue 3 (July–September,1991): 6–40.

Lefebure, Leo D. "The Wisdom of God: Sophia and Christian Theology, *Christian Century*, October 19, 1994.

Leirvik, Oddbjorn. *Images of Jesus Christ in Islam*. Uppsala: Swedish Institute of Missionary Research, 1999.

Meistermann, Barnabas. "Tomb of the Blessed Virgin Mary." In *Catholic Encyclopedia*, Vol. 14. New York: Robert Appleton Company, 1912. 22 Aug. 2010.

Merad, Ali. *Christian Hermit in an Islamic World: A Muslim's View of Charles de Foucauld*. Mahwah, NJ: Paulist Press, 1999.

Moucarry, Chawkat. *The Prophet and the Messiah: An Arab Christian's Perspective on Islam and Christianity*. Downer's Grove, IL: InterVarsity Press, 2001.

Nafisi, Azar. *Reading Lolita in Tehran: A Memoir in Books*. Random House, 2003.

Nasr, Seyyed Hossein. "Comments on a Few theological Issues in the Islamic-Chrisitan Dialogue," in Yvonne Yazbeck Haddad, and Wadi Z. Haddad, eds. *Christian–Muslim Encounters*. Gainsville: University Press of Florida, 1995, 457–67.

Nouwen, Henri J.M. *Behold the Beauty of the Lord: Praying with Icons*. Notre Dame, IN: Ave Maria Press, 1987.

Nowaihi, Mohamed al-. "The Religion of Islam. A Presentation to Christians." *International Review of Mission* 65 (1976): 216–25.

Olson, Roger E. and Christopher A. Hall. *The Trinity*. Grand Rapids, MI: Erdmans, 2002.

Packer, J. I. *Knowing God*. Downers Grove, IL: InterVarsity Press, 1993.

Parrinder, Geoffrey. *Jesus in the Qur'an*. Oxford: One World Press, 1995.

Pearson, J.D. "al-Qur'an." *Encyclopaedia of Islam* II, Vol. V, 404–5.

Rahman, Fazlur. *Major Themes of the Quran.* Minneapolis, MN: Bibliotheca Islamica, 1989.

Rice, Anne. *Christ the Lord Out of Egypt.* New York and Toronto: Alfred A. Knopf, 2005.

Robinson, Neal. *Christ in Islam and Christianity.* Albany: State University of New York, 1991.

Rubenstein, Richard E. *When Jesus Became God: The Struggle to Define Christianity During the Last Days of God.* New York: Harcourt, 1999.

Shafaat, Ahmad. "Islamic View of the Coming/Return of Jesus." http://www.islamicperspectives.com/Return OfJesus.htm.

Shams, J. D. "Jesus: God or Beloved of God?" *Muslim Sunrise*, Spring 2006, 12–18.

Skali, Faouzi. *Jésus dans la tradition soufie.* Paris: Editons Albin Michel, 2004.

Smith, Houston. "Jesus and the World's Religions." In *Jesus at 2000*, Edited by Marcus J. Borg, 107–20. Boulder and Oxford: Westview Press, 1998.

Snustad, D. Peter and Michael J. Simmons. *Principles of Genetics*, 4th ed. John Wiley & Sons, 2006.

Strobel, Lee. *The Case for Christ: A Journalist's Personal Investigation of the Evidence for Jesus.* Grand Rapids, MI: Zondervan, 1998.

Tabor, James D. *The Jesus Dynasty.* New York,: Simon & Schuster, 2006.

Thompson, James Westfall. *An Introduction to Medieval Europe 300–1500.* New York: W.W. Norton and Company, 1937.

Tyson, John R. *Who Is God in Three Persons: A Study of the Trinity.* Nashville, TN: Abingdon Press, 2005.

Vermes, Geza. *The Resurrection, History and Myth.* New York: Doubleday, 2008.

Voltaire, *A Philosophical Dictionary*, Vol. Iii — Part I.

Waseem. "Jesus Son of Mary.....Beliefs of (Ahmadiyya) Muslims," http://www.city-data.com/forum/religion-philosophy/141379-jesus-son-mary-beliefs-ahmadiyya-muslims.html.

Watt, William Montgomery. *Muslim-Christian Encounters: Perceptions and Misperceptions.* London: Routledge, 1991.

Williams, Rowan. *Arius: Heresy and Tradition*, Eerdmans, 2002.

_____. "To be worthy of the God we worship," 9/11 Speech at Al-Azhar. http://www.archbishopofcanterbury.org/1943.

Wisdom, Alan. "Guidelines for Christian-Muslim Dialogue." *Institute on Religion and Democracy,* April 2003.

Wright, N.T. *Surprised by Hope: Rethinking Heaven, the Resurrection, and the Mission of the Church.* New York: HarperCollins, 2008.

Young William P. *The Shack.* Newberry Park, CA: Windblown Media, 2007.

Young, Frances M. *Sacrifice and the Death of Christ.* London: SPCK, 1975.

Yusuf Ali, Abdallah. *The Meaning of the Holy Qur'an.* Brentwood, MD:Amana Corporation, 1989.

DISCUSSION QUESTIONS

Chapter 1

1. Can you describe the difference between "historical truth" and "mythical truth," between "absolute truth" and "contextual truth"? Are these distinctions helpful or not?

2. What is the difference between dialogue and debate?

Chapter 2

3. Compare the process for arriving at the canon of the Bible with that of arriving at the canon of the Quran. In what ways are they similar, in what ways different? Are the similarities and differences significant? If so, in what way(s)?

4. What does the term "canon" mean in this context?

5. What is the human role in the process of revelation?

Chapter 3

6. Make a list of the details derived from the three birth narratives (Matthew, Luke, and the Quran). Comparing the lists, what do the similarities and differences suggest to you?

7. Why do we know so little about the life of Jesus as a child?

8. What is the value of some of the non-canonical gospels in this regard?

Chapter 4

9. What makes a miracle a miracle?

10. Make a list of Jesus' miracles distinguishing between nature miracles and healing miracles.

11. Compare the authority with which Jesus performs miracles in the Bible to his authority to perform miracles in the Quran. Look *carefully* at the wording in both scriptures. What do you notice?

12. Why did Jesus perform miracles?

13. Can you describe the essence of Jesus' teaching in a few sentences?

Chapter 5

14. Thinking about the crucifixion as an historical event, what are the arguments for/against Jesus having died on the cross in both Christian and Muslim tradition? Has your position changed any with regard to the significance of the event?

15. Considering the verse in the Quran that references the crucifixion, "but they killed him not nor crucified him but so it was made to appear to them," what possible questions does the verse raise?

16. Why is the actual scene of the crucifixion absent from Muhammad Kamal Hussein's *City of Wrong*?

Chapter 6

17. Taking into account what you have read in Chapter 6, how would you describe sin? Is it different in Christianity and Islam? How do believers in each faith deal with sin?

18. What differences do you see in the story of Abraham's sacrifice of his son as told in the Bible and in the Quran? What can we learn from the similarities and the differences?

19. What does atonement mean? How is it achieved?

Chapter 7

20. Thinking of the sequence of events in Jesus' life (birth, death, resurrection, ascension, second coming) what are the most significant points of comparison between the two traditions? Has your own sense of what is most significant shifted?

21. What will be Jesus' role in the second coming?

Chapter 8

22. Can you think of any metaphor that works for you to describe "the infinity of God"? Do you see any distinction between the terms "trinity," "triunity," and "unity"? Can you think of any other term to describe the concept "God"?

23. What are some of God's attributes? Which attributes are uniquely God's and which are possibly shared by humans?

24. Discuss the role of "the perfect human."

Chapter 9

25. If "orthodoxy" means right belief, and "orthopraxy" means right practice, do you think Christianity is more one than the other? What about Islam? Explain.

26. What are God's "two great commandments"? Do they play out differently or the same in both traditions? If you are a praying person, do you think you would be able to pray with people of the other faith? Would you like to?

INDEX

ABOUT RON MESSIER

Ron Messier is Professor Emeritus in History at Middle Tennessee State University (MTSU) where he taught Islamic history and historical archaeology from 1972 to 2004. From 1992 to 2004, he was also adjunct professor of history and religious studies at Vanderbilt University, and full time Senior Lecturer from 2004 to 2008. His teaching and research focus on Islam and the history and archaeology of the Middle East and North Africa. He has won several teaching awards including the CASE Tennessee Professor of the Year Award for 1993. From 1987 to 1998, he directed the excavation of the ancient city of Sijilmasa in Morocco, famous for its gold trade and its contacts with Timbuktu. He is currently directing an archaeology project at Aghmat, near Marrakech, Morocco. Since 1992, he has been the lecturer for over thirty study tours to the Islamic world, including ten tours to Morocco, five to Israel, four to southern Spain, three to Syria and Jordan, three to Egypt, three to Tunisia, two to Turkey, one to Oman in the Persian Gulf, and two to Mali and Timbuktu.

He resides in Lascassas, TN with his wife Emily and is a member of St. Paul's Episcopal Church in Murfreesboro, TN.

Ron Messier is available for select readings and lectures. To inquire about a possible appearance you can contact him at www.TwinOaksPress.com.

LaVergne, TN USA
06 December 2010

207516LV00004B/1/P